COMING
TO NORTH
AMERICA

COMING
TO NORTH
AMERICA
From MEXICO, CUBA, and PUERTO RICO

SUSAN GARVER AND PAULA McGUIRE

DELACORTE PRESS/NEW YORK

Published by
Delacorte Press
1 Dag Hammarskjold Plaza
New York, N.Y. 10017

Excerpts from *I Am Joaquín / Yo Soy Joaquín: An Epic Poem* are reprinted by permission of Rodolfo Corky Gonzales. © 1967 by Rodolfo Corky Gonzales.

Manufactured in the United States of America
First printing

Designed by Rhea Braunstein

Photo research by Paula McGuire

LIBRARY OF CONGRESS CATALOGING IN PUBLICATION DATA

Garver, Susan.
 Coming to North America.

 Summary: Explores the immigrant experiences of Mexicans, Cubans, and Puerto Ricans in the United States.
 1. Mexican Americans—Juvenile literature. 2. Cuban Americans—Juvenile literature. 3. Puerto Ricans—United States—Juvenile literature. 4. United States—Emigration and immigration—Juvenile literature. [1. Mexican Americans. 2. Cuban Americans. 3. Puerto Ricans—United States. 4. United States—Emigration and immigration.] I. McGuire, Paula. II. Title.
 E184.M5G385   304.8′73072   81–65503
 ISBN 0–440–01459–X   AACR2

Contents

FROM PUERTO RICO

Introduction

After just four months of fighting in 1898, the Spanish-American War ended in victory for the United States. Spain lost control of the last of its colonies in the New World, and four centuries of Spanish domination in the Western Hemisphere came to an end. At one time Spain had controlled nearly all of Central and South America and the West Indies—the area known as Latin America. Its influence lives on, both in the language of the people and in the people themselves. Of various combinations of Spanish, Indian, and African descent, they are generally known as Hispanics.

Untold numbers of Hispanics have made their way to the United States—many illegally. By 1980 it was estimated that there were between twelve and fifteen million people of Spanish origin there. The United States is the fifth largest Spanish-speaking country in the world, following Mexico, Spain, Argentina, and Colombia. Hispanics are the second largest and fastest growing minority group in the country. The greatest numbers came from Mexico, Puerto Rico, and Cuba and serve as the basis for the discussion in this book.

Why did they come? What did they find? How have they adapted to life in the United States? This book explores the answers to these and other questions about the immigrant experience. In large part the story is told by the immigrants themselves. In their own words, taken from books, poems, reports, and interviews, they tell of their hopes and fears, their sufferings and successes. Although they share a common language and heritage, each nationality has had a different set of experiences.

The majority of Hispanics, three out of every five, in the United States are from Mexico. Estimates of the total population vary between seven and nine million. The first Mexicans to live in the United States were not immigrants. They did not pack their bags and move anywhere. They lived in what is now California, Texas, and other parts of the Southwest. Once part of Mexico, this area was taken over by the United States after the Mexican-American War of 1848. Despised and mistreated by American settlers, they became outcasts in their own land.

Nevertheless, thousands more Mexicans were to cross the border to join them. Driven out of their homeland by poverty and frequent uprisings, they came to the United States in search of a better life. What most of them found was a life of drudgery. Cruelly exploited by employers, the majority of Mexicans worked long hours for little pay. Squalid living conditions matched their working conditions. Although there have been some improvements in recent years, Mexicans are still the poorest people in the United States. They also have the highest unemployment and dropout rates. Many are migrant workers.

Cuban immigrants, on the other hand, have been successful economically. Many Cubans who came here after Fidel Castro took power in 1959 were well-educated professional people who could easily find jobs in the United States. As refugees from communism, they received financial help and a sympathetic welcome in the United States. So, unlike other Hispanic immigrants, they did not emigrate to escape poverty, and they do not have the option of returning home. There are a million Cubans living in the United States today.

While not immigrants, since they are citizens of the United States, the Puerto Ricans have nevertheless followed the pattern of other immigrant groups. Many of the more than two million Puerto Ricans in the United States live in the poor neighborhoods of New York City. There they suffer all the problems associated with slums—poverty, overcrowding, unemployment, drug abuse, and violence. Puerto Ricans earn the lowest wages, have the highest unemployment rate and the highest dropout rate (estimated at 80 percent) in New York City. The median income for Puerto Ricans is lower than that of other Hispanics.

There are approximately one million Hispanics in the United States who come from countries in the

Western Hemisphere other than Mexico, Cuba, or Puerto Rico. People from the Dominican Republic, Colombia, Argentina, and Ecuador appear to be in the greatest numbers. Most of these immigrants live in New York City and Miami.

The Hispanics are unusual among immigrant groups. They have preserved their language and culture for much longer than most other immigrant communities and have not shown a strong desire to become "Americanized," to lose their ethnic identity, as other immigrants have often done. This is partly because of their large numbers and high concentration in certain areas, and partly because they live relatively near to their homelands. Unlike immigrants from other countries, many Hispanics (other than Cubans) can make regular trips home, and this has helped to preserve their ethnic identity.

But perhaps most significant is their conscious desire to maintain their Spanish language and culture. The Chicano Movement has affirmed this determination. So has the work of other Hispanic activists. Their efforts have brought about bilingual education programs, wage reforms, and other badly needed measures. Through their own efforts, then, Hispanics have succeeded in maintaining their unique heritage and in becoming a part of life in the United States.

FROM MEXICO

Chapter 1

The Mexicans: A Conquered People

I am Joaquín
in a country that has wiped out
all my history,
stifled all my pride.

My knees are caked with mud.
My hands callused from the hoe.
I have made the Anglo rich.

Here I stand
    Poor in money
        Arrogant with pride.[1]

These lines from a poem by Rodolfo "Corky" Gonzales, a Mexican-American, echo the frustrations, the pain, and the futility that many of his people have lived with for generations.

For hundreds of years the Mexicans have been oppressed and discriminated against by the people who came into their land as conquerors. The story

begins with the arrival in Mexico of five hundred
Spaniards, led by the explorer Hernán Cortés, in
1519. The natives of Mexico at that time were
Indians—Mayans, Aztecs, and other tribes whose
culture could be traced back many hundreds of
years. As early as A.D. 700 the Mayans had built
large cities throughout vast areas of what is now
central Mexico and had connected them with ex-
cellent roadways. They had developed the "Long
Count Calendar" a thousand years before Europe
adopted the less accurate Gregorian calendar. The
Aztecs, flourishing five hundred years after the
Mayans, established an efficient form of picture
writing. Their master craftsmen worked in clay,
silver, feathers, and cloth. According to one of the
Spanish soldiers who came to conquer Mexico:

> The natives . . . are very skillful in everything,
> and the most clever and industrious people in
> the world. Among them are masters of all
> kinds of trades, and they need see a thing made
> only once to be able to make it themselves.[2]

When the Spaniards arrived, the Aztec capital of
Tenochtitlán (now Mexico City) was a thriving
commercial and political center. From there the
Emperor Montezuma II ruled a highly structured
empire.

> . . . there were and still are many beautiful
> houses belonging to the lords. They were so
> large and had so many rooms, and gardens on
> the rooftops as well as below, that they were a

sight to behold. I went inside one of the houses of the great lord [Montezuma] more than four times for no other reason than to look at it, and each time I walked so much that I became tired, but I never saw all of it. . . . In one of the houses there was a hall large enough to hold more than three thousand people comfortably. . . . The city . . . has large and very beautiful squares where every article in use among the people is offered for sale. . . .[3]

The Spanish conquest of Mexico is one of the most remarkable feats of all time. With only five hundred men, Cortés succeeded in subduing a nation of millions. This was due, in part, to the fact that the ruling Aztecs, who were despised by many of the other Indians, were engaged in putting down civil wars. The Spanish found allies in some of the anti-Aztec groups. Furthermore, the Spaniards were equipped with firearms and horses (neither of which had ever been seen before) and knew of advanced fighting techniques, such as the ambush described by Cortés in a letter to the King of Spain:

. . . [our] infantry and horsemen began retiring through the square. . . . The enemy rushed out, yelling as if they had gained the greatest victory in the world, and [our] nine horsemen feigned to charge them across the square and then suddenly to fall back; and, when [our men] had done this twice, the enemy acquired such fury that they pressed up to the very croups of the horses and were thus decoyed towards the end of the street where the ambush was laid. When we saw [our men] had passed ahead of us, and heard the shot of a gun fired which was the signal agreed upon, we knew that the time to sally forth had arrived; and, with the cry of "Señor Santiago!" we suddenly fell upon [the enemy], and rushed forward into the square with our lances, overthrowing and stopping many. . . . In this ambush more than five hundred, all of the bravest and most valiant of [the enemy's] men were killed. . . . The victory God was pleased to give us that day was one of the principal causes why the city was taken sooner, for the natives were dismayed by it. . . .[4]

The Indians thought the men with ships, guns, and horses were gods, and therefore invincible. This belief gave Cortés and his small band of men the advantage they needed. They quickly subdued the native Indian population and established Spanish rule that was to last three hundred years.

Spanish, rather than the native Indian languages, became the official language of Mexico. The customs and culture of Spain were forced on the native population. Many of their ancient religious temples were destroyed. Catholic missionaries set out to convert the Indians to Catholicism, the official religion of Spain. For the most part the missionaries were sincere in their efforts at conversion, but their techniques were often heavy-handed. For example, they were known to use imprisonment as a means of persuading the Indians to renounce their religion. Spanish civilians were often even harsher in their treatment of the Indians. They wanted the Indians' land, their gold and silver, and they felt that as conquerors it was their right to take it. They forced the Indians to work for them, building the houses and churches in the settlements, farming the land, and working in the mines. Although slavery was banned as early as 1542, the Indians remained virtual slaves for hundreds of years. Often, for example, the Indians were paid wages, but not enough to live on. They had to borrow from their employers in order to survive, and their debts were passed on from father to son. In this way they were forced to stay where they were for generations. This practice continued into the twentieth century on some *haciendas,* or estates.

The Mexico that the Spanish took over was a vast country, including what is today the Southwestern United States. The Spaniards who came to Mexico over the years came in search of gold and silver or were attracted there by the availability of land. In some cases wealthy Spanish aristocrats came to claim large parcels of land which had been given or sold to them by the King of Spain.

For these Spaniards the move to the New World was relatively easy. They came well equipped for their new life and suffered none of the hardships normally associated with settling in a strange land. One Spanish landowner had this to say about the pioneering life in California:

No one need suppose that the Spanish pioneers of California suffered many hardships or privations, although it was a new country. They came slowly and were well-prepared to become settlers. All that was necessary for the maintenance and enjoyment of life according to the simple and healthful standards of those days was brought with them. They had seeds, trees, vines, cattle, household goods and servants, and in a few years their orchards yielded abundantly and their gardens were full of vegetables. Poultry was raised by the Indians and sold very cheaply. . . . Beef and mutton were to be had for the killing, and wild game was very abundant.[5]

During the three hundred years of Spanish domination there was intermarriage among the Spaniards, Indians, and blacks (who had been brought from Spain as slaves). A caste system developed with the European-born Spanish at the top. Next were the Creoles, who were born in the New World and were of European descent. Mestizos (persons of white and Indian descent) and mulattoes (persons of white and Negro ancestry) were in the next rank. Indians and blacks were at the bottom.

The Catholic Church became as powerful in Mexico as the Spanish government. Catholic priests established missions which, in time, became large income-producing "corporations," using Indian labor the way the private landowners did. The missions expanded to include farmlands, grazing lands, and trade shops. The Church in Mexico became wealthy and worldly.

With all the strong influences the Spanish left on the region, in fact few Spaniards had immigrated to America by the end of the eighteenth century. Only six hundred were living in California at the time, and few others elsewhere. The Spanish king was not as much interested in colonizing as he was in obtaining gold.

The native Mexican resented the power of the Church and of the few Spanish landowners. For generations the Mexicans slaved for them, getting little, if anything, in return. Then in the early 1800s, revolutionary ideas began to take root. By that time the North Americans and French had both staged successful revolutions in their countries, so why not the Mexicans too? They found a champion in Miguel Hidalgo y Castilla. In 1810 he proclaimed "Long live Our Lady of Guadalupe, down with bad government, down with the Spaniards." The Mexican war for independence began. It went on for eleven years, but finally, in 1821, the people of Mexico gained control of their land.

That control was to be short lived. Soon after the Mexicans gained their independence, North American (Anglo) settlers began to move into California and other Mexican territories. That these lands belonged to Mexico was of little concern to the settlers. They believed that Americans from the United States had the right to control all the land from the Atlantic to the Pacific oceans. A New

York newspaper expressed the popular idea of "manifest destiny to overspread, to possess the whole of the continent which Providence has given us for the development of the great experiment of liberty and federated self-government."[6]

At first the Anglos were encouraged to settle in northern Mexico. The Mexican government wanted more settlers to help control the frontier Indians who resented the encroachment of the Church on their religion and the increase in taxes. Immigrants from the United States began to arrive in Mexico in increasing numbers and to occupy some of the best lands. So many came that by the late 1820s Mexicans were deeply concerned about the amount of land falling into foreign hands. A Mexican surveyor who visited Texas in 1828 reported that:

> The Americans from the north have taken possession of practically all the eastern part of Texas, in most cases without the permission of authorities. They immigrate constantly, finding no one to prevent them, and take possession of the *sitio* [location] that best suits them without either asking leave or going through any formality other than that of building their homes.[7]

The Mexican plan for the settlement of their land in the Southwest backfired. The Anglos had pledged loyalty to Mexico to be able to move onto Texas land. But having done this, they proceeded to break Mexican laws, including the one against slavery. They refused to pay their taxes, and they were contemptuous of the Mexicans. A contemporary Mexican author wrote:

> To the Texas colonists, the word *Mexican* is, and has been, an execrable word. There has been no insult or violation that our countrymen have not suffered, including being jailed as "foreigners" in their own country.[8]

By 1830 the power of the Anglos had become so strong that the Mexican government issued a decree forbidding any more arrivals. Six years later the settlers in Texas—mostly Anglos—decided that they wanted to be free of Mexican rule. They staged a revolt. For almost two weeks a small band of Texans held off a Mexican army of thousands at the Alamo, an old mission near San Antonio. Finally the Mexicans, led by the president of Mexico, General Antonio López de Santa Anna, managed to enter the Alamo, and all the Texans were killed. The defense of the Alamo rallied the Anglo Texans, and their battle cry became "Remember the Alamo!" Two months later they captured Santa Anna. The war for Texas independence had been won.

The loss of Texas was the first major step toward the Mexican decline of power in the Southwest. In other regions held by the Mexicans, Anglo traders and pioneers moved ever westward into new frontier land and were seen as strong threats to Mexican control. These pioneers said they were not just seeking the wealth of the West; they were also fulfilling God's will by moving westward.

When the United States annexed Texas in 1845, disputes over the boundary between Texas and Mexico led to war between the United States and Mexico in 1846. Less than a year and a half later, the United States Army marched victoriously into Mexico City. The war ended in 1848 with the signing of the Treaty of Guadalupe Hidalgo.

Under the terms of the treaty, Mexico was forced to give up about 500,000 square miles of territory, including what are now the states of California, Nevada, and Utah, and parts of Colorado, Wyoming, Arizona, and New Mexico. But what was to become of the Mexican inhabitants of these areas, those people of Spanish-Indian descent who had lived there for generations? According to the treaty:

> Those who shall prefer to remain in the said territories may either retain the title and rights of Mexican citizens, or acquire those of citizens of the United States. . . . and those who shall remain . . . after the expiration of [one] year, without having declared their intention to retain the character of Mexicans, shall be considered to have elected to become citizens of the United States.[9]

Most Mexicans living in the areas that Mexico had lost to the United States cared more for their land than about changes in government. They stayed where they were; their rights had been assured by the treaty. But in fact the Anglos expressed doubts about granting full civil rights to a people who spoke a foreign language and had an alien culture. Alien to whom? Certainly not to the thousands of Spanish-speaking people who had lived in these areas for centuries. They were alien to the Anglos, who came to the newly acquired territories in ever-increasing numbers to take advantage of the jobs and money there. To the Anglos, the Mexican was the outsider. The people who became Mexican-Americans with the signing of the treaty of Guadalupe Hidalgo soon found themselves outcasts in their own land.

Chapter 2

Broken Promises

Americans from the North had been convinced, during the two years of war with Mexico, that it was their "manifest destiny" to extend the United States from shore to shore. They were equally convinced that the Mexican people were inferior, with a language, traditions, and style of life not worth keeping. They saw themselves as saviors of the Mexicans, as this 1847 newspaper editorial shows:

> But we owe it as a duty to ourselves and the general cause of freedom, to keep our flag flying . . . till the progress of time, and the silent effect of our presence, our customs, our busy commerce, our active intelligence, our press, shall have breathed a new life into this unfortunate country. . . .[1]

Armed with such convictions, the North Americans saw little need to respect the rights of the Mexican people once the war had ended. Many Anglos chose to ignore the Treaty of Guadalupe

Hidalgo. Any land that they wanted they took, regardless of whether they had a right to it.

In 1848 gold was discovered in California. Thousands of gold seekers went west to claim a share of it. The Mexican natives of California, who had as much right as anybody else to stake claims, were pushed out by armed men. Also the California Foreign Miners' Tax of 1850 stipulated that foreigners (which included Mexicans) must pay a license fee in order to look for gold. That fee was so high that few Mexicans could afford to pay it. The law was eventually repealed, but Anglos continued to abuse the Mexicans. Their behavior was condemned by the historian Josiah Royce:

> Ours were the crimes of a community, consisting largely of honest but cruelly bigoted men, who encouraged the ruffians of their own nation to ill-treat the wanderers of another, to the frequent destruction of peace and good order. We were favored of heaven with the instinct of organization; and so here we organized brutality, and, so to speak, asked God's blessing upon it.[2]

Royce related the twisted view that the Anglo miners had of the Mexicans:

> He [the Mexican] had no business, as an alien, to come to the land that God had given us. And if he was a native Californian, a born "greaser," then so much the worse for him. He was so much the more our born foe; we hated

his whole degenerate, thieving, land-owning, lazy, and discontented race.[3]

At times Anglos even went so far as to execute Mexicans, concealing their actions under the guise of a fair trial:

> Any mysterious outrage was attributed to "Mexicans;". . . . It was . . . considered safe by an average lynching jury in those days to convict a "greaser" on very moderate evidence, if none better could be had. . . .[4]

Despite the mistreatment of Mexican-Americans living in the United States, thousands more Mexicans crossed the border from Mexico. Driven out by poverty, they came to California filled with hopes of finding gold or, failing that, of finding work in the mines. Many of these newcomers brought a knowledge of mining techniques that, they felt, would assure them of getting good jobs. However, their skill gained them little more than low wages and poor working conditions. A visitor to the quicksilver mines at New Almaden, California, in 1857 described the operations there:

> We enter the car and in a few moments are rumbling along this under-ground railroad, with no sound to break the silence besides the heavy breathing of our human propellers, who, with swarthy visage lighted up by the dim rays of the candles, seem almost ghastly as they bend to their work. The laborers are all Mexicans and have generally served a sort

of apprenticeship in the silver mines of Spanish America. . . .

The mechanics, who are mostly Americans, receive full city wages—from five to seven and the laborers from two to three dollars a day. These last are fair specimens of the reckless, improvident Spanish-American race. . . . It is of little consequence how much or little they receive.[5]

Besides losing mining claims that were rightfully theirs, Mexicans also lost farm and ranch lands in the Southwest. These tracts of land, sometimes as large as fifty thousand acres, had been given or sold to Spanish and Mexican settlers (in total disregard of original native American ownership) under land grants from Spain, and later from Mexico. Their ownership was guaranteed by the Treaty of Guadalupe Hidalgo. As United States control grew, however, Mexican property rights were challenged. Congress created a land commission in 1851 to review property claims. In most cases it ruled against the Mexican property owners whose land parcels were ill defined and often unrecorded. Brought into question were makeshift boundary landmarks which allowed squatters or neighboring landowners to trespass on land claims. The plight of one unfortunate Mexican landowner was described in an 1857 magazine article. His situation was by no means unusual:

His [the landowner's] ranch brought serious evils upon him. It was the seat of a multitude

of squatters, who . . . were his bitter enemies.
. . . they fenced in his best land; laid their
claims between his house and his garden;
threatened to shoot him if he should trespass
on their enclosure; killed his cattle if they
broke through the . . . fences; cut down his
valuable shade and fruit trees, and sold them
for firewood. . . .[6]

A great many land ownership disputes were
brought before the courts. Some of them took as
long as thirty years to resolve, but the results were
usually the same. Most of the disputed property
wound up in the hands of the Anglos. One reason
for this was the prohibitive cost of defending rights,
as one contemporary observer explained:

Although the treaty of Guadalupe Hidalgo
imposed on the North Americans an obligation
to respect established rights, the Americans,
always astute and filled with cunning, placed
the owners of valuable lands in such a position
that they often saw themselves obliged to
expend the value of their properties to obtain
valid titles to them.[7]

Even when a Mexican won his case in one court,
the verdict could be overturned in a higher court.
Sometimes a fair trial was out of the question.

. . . these legal thieves, clothed in the robes of
the law, took from us our lands and our houses
and without the least scruple enthroned themselves in our homes like so many powerful

kings. For them existed no law but their own will and caprice, they recognized no right but that of force. It was our misfortune that these adventurers of evil law were so numerous that it was impossible for us to defend our rights in the courts, since the majority of the judges were squatters and the same could be said of the sheriffs and the juries. I believe it would be superfluous to say that to all these, justice was only a word used to sanction robbery.[8]

The hatred that built up on both sides during the Mexican War and in the years that followed led to more violence. In 1856, for example, Los Angeles was threatened by a serious conflict between Mexican and Anglo residents. One newspaper described the year as a "strange, curious, excitable, volcanic, hot, windy, dusty, thirsty, murdering boldly, lynching, robbing, thieving season."

Violence in Texas was even more devastating. The Cart War erupted in 1857 when Anglos decided to take over the profitable Mexican hauling business between San Antonio and Chihuahua, Mexico. They brutally attacked the ox-cart drivers. The Mexican government protested and United States troops had to be brought in to provide escorts for the drivers. Twenty years later the Salt War began in a Texas salt mine worked by Mexicans and Mexican-Americans. For some years the workers had been allowed to take home enough salt for their personal use. Then a new owner took control and discontinued this policy. His decision led to

violent scenes, but when the war ended, the
Mexicans had failed to regain their right to free salt.

The hatred between Mexicans and Anglos is seen
most vividly in the accounts of Mexican bandits
who fought against Anglo injustices. One Mexican
who became an outlaw when he avenged an un-
deserved attack on one of his countrymen was Juan
Cortina, later regarded by Mexicans as a folk hero.
He stated in a proclamation to the Mexican-
Americans of South Texas on November 23, 1859:

> Mexicans! When the State of Texas began to
> receive the new organization which its
> sovereignty required as an integral part of the
> Union, flocks of vampires, in the guise of men,
> came and scattered themselves in the settle-
> ments, without any capital, except the corrupt
> heart and the most perverse intentions. . . .
> Many of you have been robbed of your
> property, incarcerated, chased, murdered, and
> hunted like wild beasts because your labor was
> fruitful, and because your industry excited the
> vile avarice which led them. . . . My part is
> taken; the voice of revelation whispers to me
> . . . that the Lord will enable me . . . to fight
> against our enemies. . . .[9]

But Mexicans who took up the fight against the
Anglo enemy stood little chance of success. Cali-
fornians and Texans formed vigilance committees.
These stopped at nothing to rid themselves of undesirable Mexicans. The committees organized
manhunts to track down and execute offenders.

Sometimes their victims were innocent of any crime but that of being Mexican.

It may seem surprising that the Mexicans living in the Southwest did not just give up and retreat over the border to Mexico. But Mexico in the late 1800s had little to offer them. Following the war with the United States the country was rocked by years of civil war. The economy was crippled, and the majority of Mexicans lived in poverty. In 1876 President Porfirio Díaz came to power. As a dictator, he managed to restore order. But he did nothing to alleviate the poverty of the masses, preferring to bestow his favors on the wealthy landowners.

The poor, it seemed, were destined to remain that way. Even simple requests for village schools were turned down or left to wither away by the government. Ernesto Galarza wrote in *Barrio Boy:*

Like many other mountain pueblos, Jalcocotán had no school. Once the village had sent a committee to Tepic to petition the government for a teacher. The committee assured the government that the neighbors would be willing to build the school themselves and to provide the teacher with a place to live. Once in a great while, when the *Jefe Político,* who represented the government, visited Jalco he would be asked very discreetly and courteously about the petition. The answer was always the same: "It is under consideration." Many years had passed—how many no one really knew—

and Jalco still had neither teacher nor school when we went to live there.[10]

Mexico, then, had few attractions for the Mexicans living across the border in the United States. Most decided to stay where they were and endure the hostility of the Anglos. As the years went by, and as conditions in Mexico got worse, thousands more Mexicans left their homes to join them.

Chapter 3

Dreams of Freedom and Prosperity

During the early years of the twentieth century conditions in both the United States and Mexico were ripe for a mass migration of Mexicans to the United States. North American industry, agriculture, and transportation systems in the Southwest were expanding rapidly, creating a great demand for labor, especially unskilled workers. At the same time, Mexico was in a state of turmoil. Opposition to the Díaz dictatorship came to the surface in 1910. Rebel armies succeeded in ousting Díaz, but not in achieving peace. Civil war raged for several years as government troops and rebel armies battled to win control of the country.

In the process entire villages were destroyed. The peasants who were caught up in the battle zones lived in terror. Martial law was declared, and massacres committed. One Mexican villager described how it was:

It reached the point where martial law was declared. There was no way of getting out now. At the end of 1913, and into 1914, you couldn't even step out of the village because if the government came and found you walking, they killed you.

The first village to be burned was Santa María, in 1913. . . . It was entirely destroyed. The *carrancistas* [soldiers] had burned everything. The dead were hanging from the trees. It was a massacre! Cows, oxen, pigs and dogs had been killed and the people, poor things, went about picking up rotten meat to eat. All the corn and beans were burned. It was a terrible pity.[1]

Such actions only drew more Mexicans to the revolutionary cause. One of them, Flores de Andrade, described her role in the movement:

I took charge of collecting money, clothes, medicines and even ammunition and arms to begin to prepare for the revolutionary movement, for the uprisings were already starting in some places. . . . I was able to get houses of men and women comrades to hide our war equipment. . . .[2]

But the constant turmoil also drove many Mexicans away. Immigration to the United States rose dramatically as thousands decided to leave danger and poverty behind them. Most of the immigrants were peasants, although some members of the Mexican middle and upper classes left too. They hoped to work in the United States until conditions at home stabilized.

Some of these immigrants were supporters of the revolution who had become disenchanted. Luis Murillo, who fought as a revolutionary, explained why he had left Mexico:

> The condition in which the country is now is nothing more than a killing of brothers, one by the other and now they don't even know why. . . . I said to myself that it didn't look like a government or a fight over convictions. Why should I fight now?[3]

Murillo described the conditions that he left behind in Mexico:

> I looked for work for a long time but everything had stopped, factories, mills, everybody was without work. With the farms burned there weren't even any tortillas to eat, nothing but maguey leaves. . . .[4]

To cross the border into the United States, Mexican immigrants had to satisfy certain requirements. In 1917 these included an eight-dollar head tax, a literacy test in Spanish, and a medical exam. For those who could meet these conditions, crossing the border presented no problems.

Many Mexican immigrants did not have it easy, however. Unable to scrape together the money for the train fare, they had to find some other way of getting across the border. Elisa Recinos traveled on foot more than four months with her husband and baby. They were bound for Texas, but their journey was halted in Ciudad Juárez, Mexico, where they spent six months living on charity and the occasional sale of birdcages.

> . . . they traveled when conditions were good and as they got food. They begged at small farms if they weren't able to sell cages and some people gave them something to eat for breakfast and supper. At some places they were given a place where they could sleep. They brought a quilt and some blankets and capes to cover their bodies while they slept, to keep out the cold.[5]

Some who could not pay the eight-dollar head tax tried to cross the border illegally. Sometimes they were caught and sent back, but many went unnoticed. Those who made it to the United States and who were able to find steady work were, at first at least, satisfied with their new life. Although Mexican immigrants were generally paid less than members of any other ethnic group similarly employed, they earned five or six times more than they had in Mexico. They could live in relative comfort with enough money for education, recreation, consumer goods, and savings. One immigrant spoke of the opportunities he found in the United States:

> I arrived . . . in 1918 when there was almost no trouble about immigration. . . . I got a job as a cleaner in a stockyard in Los Angeles

and I have been well off there, earning $35 a week. When I had saved a little money I sent for my sister and put her in school. Now she can speak English and is getting a business training. . . .

I don't want to go back to Mexico because I couldn't earn there what I am used to earning in Los Angeles and besides, one can buy more things with a dollar than with a Mexican peso.[6]

Clearly, life north of the border had great attractions for many Mexican immigrants. Martha Morales, who immigrated in 1923, realized just how much her life had changed when she went back to Mexico to visit friends:

I went [back] when I was single. Naturally if you're single and you bring money from the States, it's beautiful. . . . I went right to the same house where we had been so poor. And I kind of remembered, and now it was different. . . . I had money to buy things with. . . . Before we'd just look. . . .[7]

Life in the United States, then, was a lot easier for some Mexicans than the life they had left behind. Nevertheless, many still hoped to return home one day. Some immigrants who did go back to Mexico were disappointed in what they found there:

I have been in this country for three years and a half, for even though I went to Aguascalientes to see my parents about a year

and a half ago I didn't stay more than a
month. It had been my purpose to stay at
home and work there but I found everything
changed and dull, in other words different
from this country, and now I like it better here
and if I were to go back to Mexico it is only
to visit a while and then return.[8]

For Mexicans who decided to settle in the United
States, the adjustment to the new country was often
difficult. Most of them wanted to retain some of
their Mexican traditions, yet at the same time they
wanted to be accepted as North Americans. As
Martha Morales discovered when she went to
school, this was not going to be easy:

We came in June 1923. . . . And we tried to
learn English as fast as we could, which we
did. . . . It was no disgrace to be poor. . . .
We were Mexicans, there was no way to beat
it. In fact our skin color is different, our cultures were different. [We had] to accept it
and be proud. . . . That's the way we were
raised.

So when we went to school if anybody
called us greasers, or [said], "You eat tortillas"
. . . they were saying the truth. Because we
did have tortillas and we did have beans . . .
so we learned not to get mad. It hurt . . . but
we just grew up that way.

I do remember . . . my teacher did tell me
not to wear my bow to school. And it kind of
broke my heart because I had been raised

with a bow in my hair. . . . We tried to excel in our studies. That was our way of recompensing. . . . Even though we were proud to be Mexican, we figured they'll leave us alone about tortillas and frijoles if maybe we can do better than the next person.[9]

Determination like this helped many Mexicans to adapt to their new life and make their way in the United States. By the late 1920s some had saved enough money to establish small businesses.

In some parts of the Southwest young Mexicans began to leave the undesirable parts of town in which they had first settled, and to move into districts where their children could attend "American" public schools. In every way they wanted to live exactly like other North Americans. The Mexicans who managed to establish businesses or move into Anglo neighborhoods were, however, exceptions. For the majority of Mexican immigrants life in the United States was a struggle to survive. Underpaid, always on the move in search of work, and living in deplorable conditions, most Mexicans had no chance to better themselves.

Chapter 4

A Dream Turns Sour

Although some Mexicans found a comfortable life in the United States, most immigrants had a difficult time finding places to live and steady jobs. Those who moved into cities usually settled in the *barrios* —districts where other Mexicans had already settled. A *barrio* in Sacramento was described by an immigrant resident as

> . . . a neighborhood of leftover houses. The cheapest rents were in the back quarters of the rooming houses, the basements, and the run-down rentals in the alleys. . . .
>
> *Barrio* people . . . cut out the ends of tin cans to make collars and plates for the pipes and floor moldings where the rats had gnawed holes. Stoops and porches that sagged we propped with bricks and fat stones. To plug the drafts around the windows in winter, we

cut strips of corrugated cardboard and wedged them into the frames. With squares of cheese-cloth neatly cut and sewed to screen doors holes were covered and rents in the wire mesh mended.

Such repairs, which landlords never paid any attention to, were made *por mientras,* for the time being or temporarily. It would have been a word equally suitable for the house itself, or for the *barrio.* We lived in run-down places furnished with seconds in a hand-me-down neighborhood all of which were *por mientras.*[1]

The need to work was uppermost in the minds of the immigrants. Jobs were often difficult to find, especially when the workers could not speak or read English. They relied on the *barrio* grapevine for information.

The password of the *barrio* was *trabajo* [work] and the community was divided in two—the many who were looking for it and the few who had it to offer. Pickers, foremen, contractors, drivers, field hands, pick and shovel men on the railroad and in construction came back to the *barrio* when work was slack, to tell one another of the places they had been, the kind of *patrón* [boss] they had, the wages paid, the food, the living quarters, and other important details.[2]

Finding work became a lot easier for Mexicans after the outbreak of World War I. Many Anglos who had worked as unskilled laborers on farms and railroads left their jobs to work in the factories making arms and combat equipment. This created a gap in the labor market which Mexican immigrants could fill.

As the war went on, the need for additional labor rose. Under pressure from employers, the United States government relaxed the immigration laws for Mexicans, doing away with the entry fee and literacy test. Lured by promises of steady work and good wages, more Mexicans came to the United States.

One of the greatest needs was for seasonal farm labor in the Southwest. Mexicans were employed by the thousands to perform this backbreaking work. Moving from farm to farm, they supplied the extra hands that were needed at planting and harvesting time. As one observer put it, they did the "stooping, bending, kneeling, crawling in the dust, in the hammering rays of the southwestern sun—that work they [the Anglos] declined."[3] For this the Mexicans received paltry wages and appalling living conditions.

North American farmers, interested only in getting the most work for the least money, were generally pleased with their Mexican laborers. Commented one group of Texas farmers:

> You can't beat them as labor. They are the best labor we have. I prefer Mexican labor to

other classes of labor. It is more humble and you get more for your money. The Mexicans have a sense of duty and loyalty.[4]

The Mexicans don't live on hardly anything—tortillas and beans and a little meat—you can put 30 of them in a house, and they cook out over an open fire. The whites want a kerosene stove, and longer picking sacks, etc.[5]

The Mexicans had to be docile and humble. They were so desperate for work that they couldn't afford to argue with employers and risk losing their jobs. An immigrant who worked as a fruit picker in southern California described the evils of hiring:

Like all the others, I often went to work without knowing how much I was going to be paid. I was never hired by a rancher, but by a contractor or a straw boss who picked up crews in town and handled payroll. The important questions that were in my mind—the wages per hour or per lug box, whether the beds would have mattresses and blankets, the price of meals, how often we would be paid—were never discussed, much less answered, beforehand. Once we were in camp, owing the employer for the ride to the job, having no means to get back to town except by walking and no money for the next meal, arguments over working conditions were settled in favor of the boss.[6]

If they wanted to receive any pay at all, the workers often had to put up with employers who cheated them. The workers had no recourse. Even the police, the *autoridades,* were on the side of the employer.

> The worst thing one could do was to ask for fresh water on the job, regardless of the heat of the day; instead of iced water, given freely, the crews were expected to buy sodas at twice the price in town, sold by the contractor himself. He usually had a pistol—to protect the payroll, so it was said. Through the ranchers for whom he worked, we were certain that he had connections with the *Autoridades,* for they never showed up in camp to settle wage disputes or listen to our complaints or to go for a doctor when one was needed.[7]

The lack of all employee rights resulted in ridiculously low wages. A letter to *The Nation* magazine reported the plight of berry pickers in California during the 1920s:

> Working conditions among these laborers have been intolerable for many years. Wages by the hour were 10 cents and less. Piece work was common; the price for picking a crate of berries, 19 to 30 cents, depending on the variety, and this seldom netted the picker more than 90 cents a day. Hours were long; ten hours were standard, twelve were more often the rule. In El Monte, the center of the berry-

growing region, a system of virtual peonage prevailed.[8]

California and Texas were not the only states that needed migrant farm workers. Every year thousands of Mexican immigrants left the Southwest for a few months to go and work in the sugar-beet fields of Ohio, Wisconsin, Michigan, and other northern states.

The journey north was often a terrible ordeal. Fifty or more people would be herded together in an open truck for a journey of more than fifteen hundred miles. Reported one traveler:

> Passengers had to stand all the way and one man tied himself upright to a stake so he would not fall out if he should happen to fall asleep.[9]

Another traveler described how the workers had to resort to violence to ensure their own safety:

> The weather was cold and rainy. There were no seats in the truck; it had no top; the roads were bad; and the brakes on the truck were functioning badly. The workers finally forced the driver, at the point of a gun, to stop and buy brake fluid with money which they lent him.[10]

Those who traveled north in their own cars also faced uncomfortable journeys. Very often their cars were old, in need of repair, and dangerously over-crowded, usually with relatives. Even for citizens of the United States, the trip was far from easy.

Many . . . are native-born citizens, but since they were delivered in birth by nonregistered midwives in faraway rural counties in Texas, they find it difficult to establish their citizenship. Even the native-born citizens, in many cases, do not speak English, and they have much trouble satisfying their questioners. . . . Usually they are scared stiff for fear they won't make it to Michigan or that they will be turned back somewhere along the line.[11]

But the hardships of the trip were trivial compared with the life that awaited the workers in the North. The Department of Social Welfare in Michigan revealed its findings on the housing of migrant workers:

These people are living in a colony of dilapidated shacks on the property of the sugar company and inside the corporation limits of the village. The majority of them consist of only two small rooms and are in a filthy condition full of vermin and without sanitation. . . . Each of these houses is occupied by one to three families. In one instance there were fourteen people and only one bed. There is an inadequate number of outdoor toilets. None of them has probably ever been cleaned or limed.[12]

In one case twenty-seven people were discovered living in a single house, and in another an eight-by-twelve-foot trailer housed a family of ten. These overcrowded and unsanitary conditions led to a high incidence of disease and a higher than normal death rate among members of the Mexican colony.

A report on a family of six, responsible for seven acres of sugar beets, stated that:

> . . . these people averaged about $8.00 per week and live on about $1.00 worth of food-stuffs per week per person, which is the average credit extended to them by the company. As a rule they work from 5 A.M. until sundown in the field.[13]

Greedy employers took excessive deductions from the workers' wages. In one case a family of ten, responsible for twenty-five acres of beets, was paid only five dollars and told that "nothing more was due until after harvesting." In another instance a social worker reported that two dollars was paid for thirty-two hours of work.

Not all Mexicans returned to the Southwest when the picking season was over in the North. Some stayed on in northern industrial areas, seeking steady employment and better wages. Mills, factories, and railroads, eager to benefit from a labor force that accepted low wages and was not unionized, began to take on Mexican workers. For some Mexicans the struggle for survival was over. Others, however, found life in the northern cities even worse than before. At least in Texas they had been warm. A reporter described their plight:

When the season in the beet fields ended, friends told of opportunities of work in Chicago, so instead of returning to Texas, they came here. Mr. J found work as a track laborer. . . . The cold weather came and Mr. J was laid off, along with other track laborers. Meagre savings were exhausted, summer clothing was inadequate, illness followed, and one child died of pneumonia. Gladly they would have returned to sunny Michoacan at that time. . . . They accept their misfortunes with a sweet gentle melancholy born of generations of hardships.[14]

As earlier Chinese had been the major source of labor to build the Central Pacific Railroad, so did the Mexicans help to build the Southern Pacific and Sante Fe railroads. The railroad companies, like other employers, took advantage of the Mexicans' need for work. They paid their Mexican workers less than anyone else and provided squalid, make-shift housing. One Mexican railroad worker reported:

It [the house] had one room and a very small kitchen. The ten of us lived there for eight months, in one room. In Mexico we had four rooms. It was a dirty house, and although the Company was to furnish the house there was not a single mattress, only sacks on the beds. All of us could not lie down at once. We slept in turns. We had never done this in Mexico.[15]

Eventually the work on the railroads was completed. Some Mexicans returned to Mexico, but others stayed on in the United States, hoping to find other work. Because of anti-Mexican feelings many doors were closed, so they were usually obliged to take the lowest-paying, most unpleasant jobs. During the 1920s, in recognition of the plight of many Mexican-Americans, various organizations worked to assist them. Clinics and community centers were established in Mexican neighborhoods to help the poor and sick. The YMCA launched a program to promote better understanding between North Americans and Mexicans. And in 1929 the League of United Latin-American Citizens was established. Organized to fight discrimination against Mexican-Americans, the league sought to provide equal rights in education and employment as well as equal protection under the law. It encouraged Mexican-Americans to learn English and to vote in elections for people who would represent them.

Despite all the efforts to improve their lot, most Mexican-Americans saw little change. Migrant workers continued to move from farm to farm. City dwellers continued to live in the squalid *barrios*. Mexicans had contributed much to the prosperity of the United States by working on the farms, on the railroads, and in industry during the early years of the twentieth century. Yet they were, for the most part, kept from enjoying this prosperity. Worse was to come, for in 1929 the American economy collapsed and the Great Depression began.

Chapter 5

"America for the Americans"

When the Americans from the North moved into Mexican territory in the early 1800s, they looked down on the Mexican people. As the years went by, this contempt showed itself in the way United States employers treated Mexican laborers. When the United States needed workers, they encouraged emigration from Mexico but gave the Mexicans the worst jobs at the lowest pay. Mexican farm workers were laid off as soon as a job was done and were constantly on the move. The majority of Mexican immigrants ended up living in makeshift shanty-towns and *barrio* slums.

There were some North Americans who believed that the Mexicans preferred this way of life, as one reporter described:

> . . . they are unsettled as a class, move readily from place to place, and do not acquire or lease land to any extent. But their most un-

favorable characteristic is their inclination to form colonies and live in a clannish manner. Wherever a considerable group of Mexicans are employed, they live together, if possible, and associate very little with members of other races. . . . In the cities their colonization has become a menace.[1]

Even those Mexicans who managed to save enough money to move to a good part of town suffered from discrimination. In an interview a Mexican woman spoke about a neighbor's experience:

> They bought a new stucco house, but there is a very bad American who lives next door. The American says bad things to her, and calls her a "dirty Mexican," and she is just as clean as clean can be. My friend only lived three months there. She was so happy with her new house, she fixed it up so cute, and it was a nice house. They planted garden, flowers, and lawn. She worked all day to make it nice, but . . . she wants to move now.[2]

As long as there was a need for cheap labor, the Mexican presence was tolerated. That need evaporated in the early 1930s. When the United States found itself in the middle of the Depression, the Mexican immigrant was no longer needed or wanted. Millions of citizens had been thrown out of work—why should Mexicans be given jobs when there weren't enough for Americans? Measures were taken to prevent Mexicans from getting the few available jobs. California, for example, passed a law in 1931 barring aliens from employment on public works projects. Signs that read "No Niggers, Mexicans, or Dogs Allowed" and "Only White Labor Employed" were posted.

The suggestion was that the Mexican go home to Mexico. Many Mexicans did return to Mexico voluntarily, in fact. In the early 1930s more returned to Mexico than immigrated to the United States. The United States government helped by tightening immigration restrictions, increasing border patrol activities, and making strong efforts to find and deport illegal aliens.

But many of the Mexicans in the United States were citizens. Although wholesale deportation was illegal, some officials suggested it. Then, some city governments who could not afford to keep so many people on welfare during the Depression days offered Mexicans their fare to the border if they would leave. Implicit was the threat that their welfare payments would be discontinued. One researcher figured out that the cost of welfare for some nine thousand Mexicans in Los Angeles for one year was $800,000. It would cost the city less than $150,000 to ship the same number to Mexico City. An arrangement was made with officials of the Southern Pacific Railroad, which agreed to transport Mexicans from Los Angeles to Mexico City for $14.70 per person. The first trainload departed in February 1931, and the trips continued for several years.

Jorge Acevedo, a victim of repatriation, described the early-morning arrival of vans in Maravilla, a Mexican-American area in Los Angeles:

> Families were not asked what they would like to take along, or told what they needed . . . or even where they were going. "Get in the truck". . . . Families were separated. . . . They pushed most of my family in one van, and somehow in all the shouting and pushing I was separated and got stuck in another van. It was a very big one with boards across it for us to sit on. Nobody knew what was happening or where we were going. Someone said, to a health station.
>
> We drove all day. The driver wouldn't stop for bathroom nor food nor water. The driver was drinking and became happier as he went along. . . . It was dark when he finally ran the truck off the road. Everyone knew by now that we had been deported. Nobody knew why, but there was a lot of hatred and anger.[3]

During the period 1900–1930, one million Mexicans immigrated to the United States. In the early 1930s, some 300,000 Mexicans and Mexican-Americans were sent back over the border. At least half of them were American-born, and therefore American citizens. Repatriation was especially hard on Mexican-Americans who were United States citizens—either naturalized or native-born. Acevedo, who was a native-born North American, was determined to return to Los Angeles, his home.

One of the reasons I made it back was because I was alone. The others who were dumped into Mexico tried to travel back across the border in families and groups. They were easily spotted and turned back. I was young and strong, and I kept walking. I traveled at night, crawling into some hole or under some brush during the day. I kept off the roads when I had to and went around the larger villages. In this way, then, I walked through the northern part of Mexico, and made my way back to El Paso, Texas.[4]

After a few months and a twenty-five-hundred-mile trip, Acevedo arrived in Los Angeles. Later he became a prominent community leader and in 1967 was appointed director of the War on Poverty in Santa Clara County, California.

The repatriation program created problems in Mexico. It took time to resettle the thousands of people who were pouring into the country every week. Reported one journalist:

> . . . in early January more than ten thousand *repatriados* camped and starved, huddled together, waiting for a kind government to provide them with transportation so that they could move on. . . . Then, later in the month, the [Mexican] government sent a train of thirty-three box cars . . . and then a second train . . . to take them south and scattered them over the country. . . .[5]

For those Mexicans who could stay on in the United States, conditions were usually appalling—inadequate relief money, poor housing, racial prejudice, and segregated schooling. Often a needy Mexican family received less assistance than a needy American one: the Mexicans "needed less." Hostility toward Mexicans and Mexican-Americans during the Depression spilled over into the school system. Many schools were segregated because of their location "near the camp" or on "the other side of the tracks." Other schools were deliberately segregated. It was said that Mexican children would be more comfortable and more confident when competing and learning only with other Mexican children. But segregation made an already tense situation worse. A Mexican who attended a segregated school said:

> In the first place it gave me the feeling of inferiority which I found hard to overcome. In the second place, it forms dislike, distrust, and even hatred of the American children. In the third place the Mexican children do not get to associate with the American children and pick up their customs, habits and vice versa. . . .[6]

Segregation caused serious problems for some second-generation Mexican-Americans. They had been denied the chance to become "Americanized." At the same time, they did not feel that they were Mexicans, for many of them had never been to

Mexico. As one writer put it, the Mexican-American is a "hybrid":

> He is unable to reconcile the ideas of the old with those of the new. He accepts some of each and discards some of each. Sometimes he is wise in his choice, sometimes he is exceedingly foolish. . . . His parents are Mexicans. His children may be American. He, himself, is neither; he is both—a hybrid.[7]

Some Mexican children did attend integrated schools, where they were forbidden to speak Spanish even when they were playing in the schoolyard. Cesar Chavez, the well-known Mexican-American labor leader, spoke of the frustration that this caused him.

> In class one of my biggest problems was the language. Of course, we bitterly resented not being able to speak Spanish, but they insisted that we had to learn English. They said that if we were American, then we should speak the language, and if we wanted to speak Spanish, we should go back to Mexico.[8]

Punishment was immediate if the teacher heard the students speaking their native language. But Chavez had no wish to give up the language and customs of his people and could not understand why he was being told to do so.

> It's a terrible thing when you have your own language and customs, and those are shattered. I remember trying to find out who I was and

not being able to understand. Once, for instance, I recall saying I was a Mexican. The teacher was quick to correct me. "Oh, no, don't say that!" she said. But what else could I say? In a nice way she said, "You are an American. All of us are Americans," and she gave me a long explanation I couldn't understand. I went home and told my mother, "Mama, they tell me I'm an American!" To me an American was a white man. My mother couldn't really give me a satisfactory answer either. She said I was a citizen, but I didn't know what a citizen meant. It was too complicated.[9]

The poor treatment of Mexicans in the United States during the 1930s finally led to action. Mexicans began to form labor unions and to demand decent wages and fair treatment. Angry employers reacted by branding union organizers as Communists and demanding that they be deported. One Mexican who suffered this fate was Jesus Pallares, who helped to organize unions at several mining camps in New Mexico. A government relief office worker described what happened next.

Attempts were made by my office to intimidate Pallares by withholding relief and by inventing reasons by which he could be removed from relief jobs. . . . threats were made to starve his family in order to involve him in an argument which the relief agency hoped would give rise to violence on his part. . . . Such violence never took place, even though situations were carefully prepared in advance such as the placing of a hammer on the supervisor's desk within his easy reach. . . . a complaint was made to Washington on the vague and flimsy basis that Pallares was a "troublemaker."[10]

During the same period in California, Mexican fruit pickers were organizing, calling for wage increases and transportation assistance. The growers' own great cooperative organization has been created as a result of the oppression and exploitation by brokers and shippers in the past. Still, they refused to accept the organization of their workers. The growers' opposition to the Mexican citrus-fruit pickers in Orange County was particularly ruthless. When the union struck, retaliation came in the form of vigilantes, strikebreakers, slanted newspaper stories, and a state motor patrol in the area to "direct law-and-order activities." The sheriff stated: "It is a fight between the entire population of Orange County and a bunch of Communists." However, dozens and dozens of non-Communist Mexican fruit pickers were jailed, including 116 who were arrested while traveling on the highway. They were charged with riot and placed under a bail of five hundred dollars each. They were held for two weeks before a judge finally released them and criticized the authorities for their actions.

During the strike, the newspapers upheld "law-abiding citizens" and carried headlines such as "Vigilantes Battle Citrus Workers in War on Reds."

Only one newspaper defended the fruit pickers. The Los Angeles *Evening News* reported:

> Be it known that the "heroic band of vigilantes," twenty-eight in number, who last Friday with clubs and tear-gas bombs stole up on a peaceful meeting of 150 Mexican fruit pickers in Placentia, fell upon the dumbfounded workers without warning, smashed jaws and cracked heads, dispersed the group save one striker smashed into unconsciousness and left lying on the ground, were exactly this:
>
> Twenty-eight Los Angeles bums, recruited from streets and beer-halls through a detective agency and paid eight dollars a day by the citrus growers to foment violence and terrorize the striking Mexican pickers.[11]

This was just one of the strikes against the California growers in the 1930s. Mostly unsuccessful and always blamed on the influence of the Communists [or "Reds"], these strikes nevertheless were laying the groundwork for successful labor organization in the future.

The years of the Depression had a strong effect on the typical North American's attitude toward immigration. Earlier slogans such as "Land of Opportunity" and "Refuge of the Oppressed" were replaced by "America for the Americans." It was not until economic conditions improved after World War II that Mexican-Americans, along with other minority groups, could begin again to claim their civil rights as United States citizens.

Chapter 6

The War Years

When the United States entered World War II in December 1941, chronic unemployment gave way to an employment boom. The country geared up for war production. There was work for anyone who wanted it. The prospects for Mexican-Americans changed. Women who had had difficulty finding even low-paying domestic work during the early thirties now found well-paying jobs in defense plants. Their husbands, brothers, and sons enlisted or were drafted into the armed services. Raul Morin, a Mexican-American author and a draftee, said:

> Army life afforded many their first experiment in putting into practice a real democracy, a simple, quiet democracy effected without any pressure or compromise. We were so engrossed in our new chores of soldier life and so aware of an uncertain future, that no room was left for anyone to be choosy about his neighborhood.[1]

Mexican-Americans served as members of the National Guard throughout the Southwest and were prominent among the volunteers and draftees. The very first draftee, selected in the National Draft Lottery in October 1941, was Pedro Aguilar Despart from Los Angeles. The recruits came from rural farmlands and from the *barrios* of the big cities; they were joined by other Mexicans who crossed the border. North Americans, aware of the discrimination that Mexicans had suffered over the years, were surprised at the number of Mexican volunteers. Many Mexican-Americans hoped that by joining the armed services, they could prove their loyalty to the United States and help put an end to discrimination. Another, less patriotic reason for joining, was expressed by Cesar Chavez:

> I don't know why I joined the navy in 1944; I think mostly to get away from farm labor. I was doing sugar beet thinning, the worst kind of backbreaking job, and I remember telling my father, "Dad, I've had it!"
>
> Neither my mother nor my dad wanted me to go, but I joined up anyway. It was wartime. I suppose my views were pretty much the views of most members of a minority group. They really don't want to serve, but they feel this awesome power above them that's forcing them to do it.[2]

Life in the armed services gave Mexican-Americans from different areas an opportunity to become acquainted and compare life-styles. They discovered a common ethnic identity and developed a spirit of unity.

> Our people have the same common spirit. Here were those individuals who had never met before, and yet at the very first contact everyone acted as though they had known each other for a long time.
>
> On the first night at the reception center, all the gang, approximately 30, as if by a prearranged plan automatically gathered outside the barracks to get better acquainted. Soon someone brought out a guitar and we began singing songs, old and new, all familiar to us. . . . The songfest kept getting louder and the tempo picking up.[3]

Mexican-Americans fought in all branches of the armed services, from the Philippines to North Africa to Europe. In proportion to their numbers they were awarded more congressional Medals of Honor than any other minority group. One group of soldiers deserves special notice. Company E of the 141st Regiment, 36th (Texas) Division, was made up entirely of Spanish-speaking soldiers, most of them from the El Paso area. They brought their Mexican traditions with them to the army:

> From Camp Bowie they started out eating together, training together . . . sleeping together . . . speaking Spanish when serious and English for military discipline. Together they enjoyed not only the regular Army chow, but also their preferred Mexican dishes which

many times were prepared by the company cooks who were also of Mexican descent.[4]

Company E quickly earned a reputation for excellence in battle skills. That reputation was put to the test when, in September 1943, the company landed at Salerno in Italy:

> They waded right into the thick of things, battling back and forth with the Nazi defenders. It wasn't long before a Mexican-American became the first hero of the whole Division. This was a big, tall, bronze-faced *Chicano* Sergeant named Manuel S. Gonzales. . . . he's from somewhere in West Texas near the Mexican border, some spot where they don't speak anything but Spanish. . . . A wonderful squad leader, he'd volunteer for anything, any time, and at Salerno, when his squad was practically wiped out, he fought a one-man battle against the Germans for 24 hours.[5]

Many other acts of heroism were performed by Mexican-American soldiers. Guy Louis Gabaldon, for example, had grown up on Los Angeles' East Side and had lived with a Japanese-American family since his early teens. He learned to speak Japanese fluently from his friends. His "foster parents" were interned early in the war.* Gabaldon,

---

* Some 117,000 Japanese-Americans, over half of whom were American citizens, were imprisoned in relocation camps in the interior of the United States during World

having just turned seventeen, decided to enlist in the marine corps. On Saipan he was assigned to Intelligence, but Galbadon found the work boring. He would sneak off into the jungle and round up Japanese as prisoners, often by simply calling out in Japanese and "promising 'em things," such as good treatment, food and water, and medical care. Some days he would bring back as many as thirty prisoners, and his buddies would make bets on the day's catch. One day he bagged seven hundred prisoners in seven hours by forcing the other Japanese prisoners to go out and bring back some more. When he was finally wounded and his fighting career was over, Gabaldon received the Silver Star "for the capture of over 1,000 enemy."[6]

The returning veterans were proud of their victorious role in Europe and the Pacific. Having proved their loyalty to the United States, they looked forward to taking their rightful place in society. Government loans for mortgages and education were made available to all honorably discharged veterans. This enabled some Mexican-Americans to purchase homes, move into other neighborhoods, establish small businesses, acquire skills, and seek good jobs.

But Mexican-Americans who had hoped that their participation in the war would help solve the

---

War II. For a more complete discussion of the episode, see *Coming to America: Immigrants from the Far East* by Linda Perrin (New York: Delacorte Press, 1980).

problems of the Mexican-American population as a whole were disappointed. During the early 1940s, while the war was still going on, gang fighting broke out in Los Angeles between Anglo and Mexican-American teen-agers. The latter, dubbed *pachucos,* sported a distinctive style of dress—the zoot suit— which was, in a sense, a badge proclaiming pride in their heritage. Octavio Paz, the Mexican poet, made a study of the *pachucos.*

> The pachucos are youths, for the most part of Mexican origin, who form gangs in southern cities; they can be identified by their language and behavior as well as by the clothing they affect. They are instinctive rebels, and North American racism has vented its wrath on them more than once. . . . But the pachucos do not attempt to vindicate their race or the nationality of their forebears. Their attitude reveals an obstinate, almost fanatical will-to-be, but this will affirms nothing specific except their determination . . . not to be like those around them. . . . [they do] not want to blend into the life of North America.[7]

As the fighting went on, local authorities and a largely hostile press whipped up anti-Mexican sentiment among Americans by biased reporting of what were often minor incidents. Despite statistics to the contrary, it was generally assumed that zoot suits were worn only by criminals. On this basis mass arrests were made. Said one Mexican-American:

"We're Americans for the draft but Mexicans for jobs and for the police."

There was delinquency among this group, but no more than in other ethnic groups. And nobody had to look far to find reasons for the unrest. One Los Angeles police officer blamed lack of employment and low wages, among other reasons. And the poor standard of living among Mexicans was largely a result of discrimination against them.

Gene Coon, in his short story "Pachuco," described what it was like to be young in the Mexican community of Los Angeles:

> [They were] a bunch of kids of Mexican ancestry, underprivileged, shunned, bitter, full of hate. . . . They wanted to get back at the Anglo-Saxon world that had made pariahs of them, and they did it in the way they knew best—breaking its laws. Stealing cars, breaking into neighborhood stores. Kids with an ancestral love for the beautiful and kind, who found no place for such love in Los Angeles' East Side.[8]

In June 1943 a fight erupted between Anglo sailors and Mexican-American youths in a Los Angeles slum. The incident mushroomed into the "Zoot Suit Riots," which involved the "invasion" of more sailors, military personnel, and civilians, who attacked any Mexican youth in sight. City police made no attempt to protect the victims. A Mexican-American student described what happened:

Police cars and ambulances with Mexican kids and some with sailors raced by. . . . This night the Shore Patrol or MPs almost never caught up with the sailors and soldiers. But the police always came along and mopped up the kids and took 'em to jail.

Filled with disgust, the student went on:

I am going to Mexico and fight in the airforce. I'll fight with Mexicans . . . not with *gabachos* [Americans]. Is this what we are fighting for? What Emilio takes his pennies and nickels to school for to buy a jeep? Democracy doesn't work at home. . . . This is like a street in Germany tonight, and you know it.[9]

Responding to protests from the Mexican government, the California authorities denied that the riot was of racial origin. However, a fact-finding committee set up by the governor of California found that racial prejudice was indeed the cause. The committee also stated that the recent increase in crime could not be blamed on the Mexicans, because delinquency among them had increased less than in other ethnic groups. Despite such statements in defense of the Mexican-Americans, despite the fact that Mexicans had fought gallantly in the war, discrimination continued. They were still paid the lowest wages, still barred from good jobs, still forced to live in slums and shantytowns. Nevertheless, hundreds of thousands more Mexicans crossed the border to work in the United States.

Chapter 7

They Came to Work

Most Mexicans who crossed the border during the war years came to work on the farms of the Southwest. A critical shortage of farm laborers had developed as people left the land to join the armed services or to work in arms factories. To ease the shortage, the United States government negotiated the Bracero ("Hired Hand") Agreement with Mexico.

Under the terms of the agreement, which was signed in 1942, Mexico allowed its citizens to work in the United States under contract for short periods. The United States, in return, accepted responsibility for the workers' transportation, health care, wages, food, and housing. The "temporary" program remained in force until 1964.

The Mexican government determined how many workers could be spared from any given area and issued exit permits. Workers then gathered at migratory stations in Mexico for approval and processing, before being sent across the border. There were far more applicants than there were permits, so it wasn't long before a bribery system developed. One *bracero* who successfully bought his way across the border on three separate occasions said:

> My government has nothing to do with this. It is merely government employees who conduct these practices. We, the braceros, are truly the guilty ones. When the . . . program first began, we would pay the government agents 5, 10, or 20 pesos—just small gifts for the sake of friendship. . . . The gifts gradually got larger and larger, and the agents began to take them for granted.[1]

Workers who were not selected in their towns descended upon the migratory stations. There they would wait, sometimes for several weeks, wondering if they would ever be chosen. One *bracero* said:

> The most galling part of the whole process is the uncertainty of it all. Men have to wait on the scene for weeks. Day after day there is no hiring. Some days hundreds of men must stand for hours under the broiling sun while the representative of some California grower selects some fifty from their number. Then there is another indefinite wait until another rancher arrives.[2]

And still more workers came to the migratory stations—camping in public parks, scavenging for food, and trying to stretch their funds until the selection process was completed. Between 1942 and 1964 more than four million contract laborers came legally to the United States to work. In addition, many Mexicans who had been denied permits crossed illegally. One Mexican explained why.

> Down in Mexico . . . they are still very poor. There are lots and lots of farmers who are still paying their workers maybe 8 pesos a day. That's about sixty-five cents. . . . The results— well, you try it. Let's say you have a wife and five or six kids, and probably your father and mother to support. . . . Well, on that kind of money you will probably be able to have only one meal a day. That is very common in Mexico.[3]

Once in the United States, the *braceros* were guaranteed at least fifty cents an hour. These workers were all men, unlike the local migrant workers who usually worked as family units. The growers were pleased to have an unorganized labor force that accepted minimum wages and one that required a minimum of housing facilities as well. A government report summed up the status of these laborers:

> The foreign migrant is indentured to a particular farmer or farm association for the duration of this contract. One grower, speaking of the Mexican farm labor program, said that "we used to own slaves, now we rent them from the government."[4]

The *braceros* were not the only cheap labor available. Another group, still in existence today, were "green carders," or commuters, who lived in Mexico and crossed the border every day to work on North American farms. A third group of laborers, also still in existence, drew the lowest wages, the least consideration, and the most publicity of all. These were the illegal immigrants, or "wetbacks"—so called because many of them waded or swam across the Rio Grande to get to the United States. Some came illegally because they could not meet the immigration requirements. Others defied the law because they did not want to wait for the necessary papers. All took great risks in the hope of finding a better life.

The journey across the border was often arranged by a professional "smuggler," who didn't care about the lives of the men he handled. One group of forty-six illegal aliens were treated not as men but as so many pieces of meat. After paying money to several people along the route, the group was put into a truck bound for Chicago:

> . . . they were locked in. They never saw the driver of the truck. Upon arrival in Chicago they were to pay another hundred dollars. . . .
>
> En route some men began to faint for lack of air, others to gasp for breath, others yelled and pounded on the walls of the truck. The driver stopped the truck and told them that he could not open the doors because he did not

have a key but that they were only thirty
minutes away from San Antonio, Texas.

Upon arrival at San Antonio at a particular
address, one or two of the aliens, in a dazed
condition, got out and walked into a neighboring yard. Two or three tried to hide in the alley
behind the garage. The neighbors called the
police about a disturbance at this address. . . .
Thirteen of the Mexicans were taken to a local
hospital. One was dead on arrival, and two
others died the following day.[5]

This was not the only such incident. Death was
accepted as a possibility in any illegal border crossing. Speaking of corpses found en route, one illegal
alien remarked:

They are dead, that's all. . . . Everybody takes
that chance in this business and when the time
comes for you, you've got what God's will has
determined and that's all.[6]

Why some Mexicans were prepared to put up
with such dangers is made clear by the experience
of one illegal alien. He had made about $500 a
year in Mexico as a tenant farmer. After being
smuggled into this country, he earned $160 a week
in a factory near Los Angeles.

Since 1968 the chances of coming legally to the
United States from Mexico have been reduced. The
immigration law that came into effect in that year
restricted the number of Mexican immigrants to
twenty thousand a year. This quota and the long

wait for a visa (about two and a half years) led many to avoid the legal process.

Illegal immigrant workers from Mexico have always been welcomed by those who employ them. Although they would be deported by immigration authorities if found, the workers have often been "protected" by their employers. They provide, after all, the cheapest possible source of labor. In 1951 the President's Commission analyzed the plight of the wetbacks:

> The wetback is a hungry human being. His need of food and clothing is immediate and pressing. He is a fugitive and it is as a fugitive that he lives. Under the constant threat of apprehension and deportation, he cannot protest or appeal, no matter how unjustly he is treated. Law operates against him but not for him. Those who capitalize on the legal disability of the wetbacks are numerous and their devices are many and various.[7]

Living in constant fear, illegal immigrants have always had to accept what they were offered— usually the worst jobs and the lowest wages.

The exploitation of Mexican illegals goes on. In 1978 a Labor Department official investigated the garment industry in New York:

> Just a few weeks ago, I interviewed a woman who is paid 1 cent a collar. . . . Working hard, she is able to make 200 collars a day. *That's $2 per day!* . . .[8]

While employers welcomed Mexican illegals, others in the United States have condemned them. The wetbacks, their critics claim, have kept wages down and taken jobs away from legal residents. Some of the loudest complaints have come from people of Mexican descent who are either legal immigrants or United States citizens. One Mexican-American student said in the 1950s:

> As long as there are people here willing to work for the incredibly low wages for which the wetbacks work, the Spanish-speaking people are forced to leave their homes, go to strange places, and seek jobs paying just wages that will enable them to provide food, clothing and shelter for their large families. These people are also forced to deprive their children of an education since these youngsters must travel and work with their parents to earn their daily living.[9]

Wetbacks have also kept alive the racial discrimination that Mexican-Americans have been trying to eliminate. A Mexican-American World War II veteran, testifying before a Senate committee on migratory issues in the 1950s, denounced the illegal workers in his community, saying their presence had accentuated racial tension.

Another serious charge against illegal aliens is that they have often been involved in drug trafficking. While there is no doubt that large quantities of marijuana and heroin have been smuggled across the border, the number of Mexicans involved in this trade is relatively small. The majority of illegal immigrants from Mexico have simply been poor people in search of work. Many of them do not consider that they have committed any crime in coming here, and they say that their only crime is being poor.

Leonel J. Castillo, a Mexican-American and commissioner of the Immigration and Naturalization Service, said:

> When you see the drive and ambition of someone who has walked 200 miles across the desert to come here to take any job, you develop a great sense of respect for them and a great question about what this country is really doing.[10]

Traditionally, illegal Mexicans looked for work in agriculture, especially in the Southwest. Since 1970, however, the picture has changed. With greater mechanization has come a decreased need for cheap farm labor. The unionization of farm laborers has also helped to shift the illegal worker to an urban rather than a rural setting. In recent years many Mexicans have migrated to San Antonio, Chicago, or Dallas.

The number of people who have entered the United States illegally is not known. Estimates range between one million and twelve million illegals, most of whom are thought to be Mexicans. It has proved impossible to know the exact number.

The numbers are likely to stay high as long as North American employers are willing to hire illegals and as long as poverty remains widespread in Mexico.

One hope is that the expanding oil industry in Mexico will affect the flow of Mexican immigrants —legal or illegal—to the United States. Mexican officials speculate that increasing oil revenues will pay for economic development. This might lead to new jobs in many areas in Mexico. They also warn, however, against optimism and any *immediate* effect on emigration. Poverty and unemployment cannot be solved overnight. The results from the investment of oil revenues—whatever they may turn out to be —may not be available till the end of the century.

Chapter 8

Mexican Heritage: A New Awareness

The 1960s and 1970s brought significant changes in the lives of many Mexican-Americans. Thanks to strong and determined leaders, who urged the people to fight for their rights and to show pride in their heritage, they made some progress. There is still a long way to go toward ending the oppression and discrimination that has kept them in poverty for decades. But the first steps have been taken.

No group was more in need of change than the farm workers. Always poorly paid, they had lacked the social and economic strength to improve their living and working conditions. But then, in the 1960s, a popular leader emerged, committed to organizing these farm workers. He is Cesar Chavez, a former migrant worker. Chavez gave up a steady, well-paying job in a worker's organization because he felt it was not doing enough for his people. He

67

was willing to give up financial security because of his outrage at the prevailing conditions.

Attempts to organize unions among farm workers date back to the late 1800s, but most of them failed. The first real success came in 1962 when Cesar Chavez organized the National Farm Workers Association in Delano, California. However, it was not until after this union struck against the grape growers in Delano in 1965 that progress was made. The workers called for the proposed federal minimum wage of $1.40 an hour (they traditionally received less than the minimum wage of other than farm workers) and for improved working conditions. Speaking of the plight of the grape workers, Chavez declared:

> . . . Some people say education will do it— write off this generation of parents and hope my son gets out of farm work. Well, I'm not ready to be written off as a loss, and farm work could be a decent job for my son with a union. But the point is that this generation of farm-labor children will not get an adequate education until their parents earn enough to care for the child the way they want to. . . . All we need is the recognition of our right to full and equal coverage under every law which protects every other working man and woman in this country.[1]

During the strike Chavez chose to attract national attention to his cause by calling for a boycott against grapes. To dramatize the boycott, Chavez and his followers made a three-week march from Delano to Sacramento in 1966. A supporter who was there to greet them said:

> Before 1965 I can say that we lived in the dark ages because we were not involved as a people, not socially aware of the problems and injustices. . . . [Then] Cesar Chavez . . . marched from Delano to Sacramento. The marchers arrived on Easter Sunday and there were ten thousand people. That was the largest group of Mexican-Americans I had ever seen. It was a beautiful experience. . . . From then on there was a new spirit among the Mexican-Americans, a new spirit of awareness and concern.[2]

The strike lasted five years—hard and difficult years. Chavez's crusade was known as La Causa. It soon took on some of the features of the anti–Vietnam War movement of the sixties. It was non-violent in nature, it used marches and other peaceful demonstrations to get across its message, and it appealed to the young. Eventually the original boycott (and later ones against the grape and lettuce growers) had an economic effect upon the growers, cutting down on the numbers still in business and the amount of acreage still in cultivation in California. Many Catholic bishops rallied to Chavez's side, and La Causa slowly gained national political recognition. By 1973 the United Farm Workers union was launched and already at battle with the older Teamsters and AFL-CIO union for contracts. There were many battles ahead. The boycott was taken abroad when the growers began dumping their unwanted produce in Europe. But the farm workers at last were organized and had a voice in their own future.

Other strikes against growers took place during this time, not always with success. But the seed of activism was sown. Luis Valdez founded and directed El Teatro Campesino. This was a theater group that performed skits to inform and inspire the grape strikers. Valdez discussed one effect of the National Farm Workers Association (the original name of the UFW).

> After years of isolation in the barrios of Great Valley slum towns like Delano, after years of living in labor camps and ranches at the mercy and caprice of growers and contractors, the Mexican-American farmworker is developing his own ideas about living in the United States. He wants to be equal with all the working men of the nation, and he does not mean by the standard middle-class route. We are repelled by the human disintegration of peoples and culture as they fall apart in this Great Gringo Melting Pot, and we are determined that this will not happen to us.[3]

Valdez's observations apply not only to farm workers but to all Mexican-Americans who became aware of their rights. Many new terms are being used to inspire ethnic pride, and old terms are taking on new significance. *La Raza*—the race of

Spanish-speaking people—indicates racial pride in their past. Today many of the younger Mexican-Americans choose to be called *Chicanos,* a form of the word *Mexicano.* The Chicanos are mainly young activists who take great pride in their Mexican heritage.

During the 1960s and 1970s Mexican-Americans began to reach out for equality in all areas—wages, living conditions, landownership, and politics. They were helped by Mexican-American leaders who were not afraid to fight for their rights. One of these leaders, former migrant worker Reies López Tijerina, attempted to reclaim for the Mexicans land that had originally been given them under Spanish land grants in what is now New Mexico. Tijerina's efforts landed him in jail, from where he protested:

> What is my real crime? As I and the poor people see it, especially the Indo-Hispanos, my only crime is UPHOLDING OUR RIGHTS AS PROTECTED BY THE TREATY OF GUADALUPE HIDALGO. . . . My only crime is demanding the respect and protection of our property, which has been confiscated illegally by the federal government. . . . I denounce those in New Mexico who have never opened their mouths at any time to defend or support the thousands who have been killed, robbed, raped of their culture. . . .[4]

Another leader who rose from being a field hand to become an influential spokesman and organizer is Rodolfo "Corky" Gonzales of Denver, Colorado. In 1965 he founded La Crusada Para la Justicia (Crusade for Justice). He explained to his followers that he did not preach violence but self-defense. The goal was to reclaim what was theirs.

The crusade calls for self-rule by Chicanos in their communities, particularly political rule. It provides cultural, social, and financial information and help, and stresses the importance of self-development in the *barrio* communities. Gonzales said:

> We are basically a communal people in the pattern of our Indian ancestors. Part of our cultural rights and cultural strengths is our communal values.[5]

For decades the American education system, by ignoring Mexican history and traditions, denied generations of young Mexican-Americans pride in their heritage and in themselves. One Chicano said:

> My early schooling was a terribly destructive experience, for it stripped away my identity as a Mexicano and alienated me from my own people, including my parents. . . . Like many Mexican-American children my school experiences made a peripheral person of me. My Anglo-white experiences at school so completely conflicted with my Mexican-brown experiences at home that I rejected one for the other only to find that I couldn't fully participate in either. . . . Most of the time I

was simply a displaced person who, in his better moments, should have realized that he was trying to be someone or something he actually was not.[6]

Frustration and confusion among Mexican-American students often led them to lose interest in education and drop out of school. In some instances their teachers made no effort to encourage them to stay. But many teachers believed that certain changes in school courses were needed. These included the introduction of Mexican history, culture, and literature, and bilingual education. They hoped this would help to lower the high dropout rate, ease hostility and frustration, and provide Mexican-American children with a better chance in life. Corky Gonzales declared:

> We don't want our 500 University students to become 500 Gringos in suburbialand. Although we became economically poor, our parents preserved our culture and traditions. With strong family ties the "New Chicano Movement" is the biggest, strongest and most powerful movement in the nation.[7]

Neither did parents want their children to forget their heritage. A concerned mother said:

> I'm very interested in the education of my children. I want them to have bilingual-bicultural educations in school. I want my children to have their education in two languages—Spanish and English. I want their

textbooks to be written by Chicanos, by Mexicans from a Mexican perspective, a Chicano perspective, not English textbooks translated into Spanish. I want my children to sing in Spanish in school and to play Spanish games. I want them to learn about Spanish art, to develop the Spanish language. The combination of the best of each culture and forming one.[8]

Finally in 1968 Congress passed the Bilingual Education Act, to encourage schools to introduce bilingual programs where appropriate. This, it was hoped, would remedy some of the problems among Mexican-American children. As it turned out, however, individual states and school districts were slow to act upon the proposal, and often ignored it altogether. Two years after the passage of the act there was no noticeable improvement in the education standards of Mexican-Americans. Some 42 percent of Mexican-American children were dropping out before finishing high school. In the same year the Senate Select Committee on Equal Education Opportunity was told:

The Mexican-American has [a lower] educational level than either black or Anglo; the highest dropout rate; and the highest illiteracy rate. These truths stand as massive indictments against the present educational system. As well, they are indictments of either negligence or intended homicide against a minority group.[9]

That some schools finally adopt bilingual education is due entirely to the efforts of Mexican-Americans. At Crystal City, Texas, for example, Mexican-American students boycotted the town's schools. Mexicans were then able to win enough seats on the school board to end its domination by Anglos, and to introduce bilingual education and other reforms. But many people felt that tax money should not be used to teach languages other than English and argued the point fiercely. Early in 1981 newly elected President Ronald Reagan announced he was going to cut funds for bilingual education from the new federal budget he was preparing.

Mexican-Americans have learned, during two decades marked by strikes, boycotts, and less militant action, that they can make their voices heard, that they can bring about reforms. Much more needs to be done to put an end to the economic oppression, lack of opportunity, and cultural isolation that many of them still suffer. But progress has been made by some groups and this has encouraged others.

Today millions of people of Mexican descent live in the United States. Many have never known anything but poverty and discrimination. But a new awareness is developing in many Mexican-American communities. It is an awareness that, as Americans, they can demand the same rights, privileges, and treatment as other Americans. But there is much more to it than that. It is an awareness that, as Mexicans, they also have a right to show pride in their heritage—to maintain a language and traditions that go back to ancient times. As one Mexican-American put it:

> What we are saying is that we want to be here, but without losing our language and our culture. They are a richness, a treasure that we don't care to lose.[10]

FROM CUBA

The North American (Anglo) settlers who moved onto Mexican lands in the nineteenth century found strong influences left by the Spanish on the region, which encompasses such states as California, Arizona, and New Mexico. This house, several hundred years old, was photographed by John Collier in Ranchos de Taos, New Mexico, in January 1943. (Courtesy of the Library of Congress.)

When the United States annexed Texas in 1845, disputes over the boundary between Texas and Mexico led to war. In one of the major battles General Zachary Taylor drove the Mexican army, commanded by General Mariano Arista, across the Rio Grande into Mexico. (Engraving. National Archives.)

Living conditions for Mexicans were often appalling. The kitchen in a Mexican house in Crystal City, Texas, 1939. (Photo by Russell Lee. Courtesy of the Library of Congress.)

During the early years of the twentieth century, conditions were ripe for a mass migration of Mexicans to the United States. For the majority of Mexican immigrants, life in the United States was a struggle to survive. Most ended up living in makeshift shantytowns and *barrio* slums. Here is a 1939 view of downtown San Antonio, Texas, with a Mexican cemetery in the middleground and a Mexican house in the foreground. (Photo by Russell Lee. Courtesy of the Library of Congress.)

The poor treatment of Mexicans in the United States during the 1930s finally led to action. Mexicans, such as these cantaloupe pickers in Imperial Valley, California, tried to help form labor unions and to demand fair wages and fair treatment. (Photo by Dorothea Lange, 1938. Courtesy of the Library of Congress.)

It was not until economic conditions improved after World War II that Mexican-Americans, such as this cotton-picker photographed in the San Joaquin Valley, California, in 1936, could begin to claim their civil rights as Americans. (Photo by Dorothea Lange. Courtesy of the Library of Congress.)

The 1942 Bracero (Helping Hand) Agreement between the United States and Mexico provided for Mexican contract labor for short periods. This trailer truck, with 127 Mexican farm workers, prepares to leave the U.S. Immigration Border Patrol headquarters at El Paso, Texas, for the Pecos Valley in New Mexico. All the workers waded the Rio Grande from Juarez after a recruiting plan collapsed. The U.S. Immigration Service abandoned efforts to halt illegal entry of Mexican farm workers and turned over thousands of *braceros* to North American employers. (U.P.I.)

Most attempts to organize unions among farm workers failed. The breakthrough did not come until 1962, when Cesar Chavez organized the National Farm Workers Association in Delano, California. A five-year strike against the growers started in 1965, and a widespread boycott of grapes resulted in national support for Chavez's crusade, *La Causa,* and the formation of the United Farm Workers Union. (Cesar Chavez, 1969. Photo courtesy of the Archives of Labor and Urban Affairs, Wayne State University.)

When the battleship *Maine* mysteriously blew up in Havana harbor in 1898, the United States intervened in the Cuban revolt against Spain. The resulting Spanish-American War lasted only four months and ended Spanish rule in the Caribbean. This photo shows the *Maine* entering Havana harbor in 1898. (National Archives.)

There had been a migration of Cuban tobacco workers to the United States in the late nineteenth century when anti-Spanish struggles ruined tobacco plantations in Cuba. These young cigarmakers, all under fourteen, worked in Tampa, Florida, in 1909. (Photo by Lewis Hine. National Archives.)

In 1961, Castro declared he was a Marxist-Leninist and, in the face of United States opposition, strengthened his political and economic ties to the Soviet Union. Castro is shown here greeting heads of state of "nonaligned nations" arriving for a conference in Havana in 1979. (U.P.I.)

Since 1959, some 600,000 disaffected Cubans have entered the United States as exiles. At first, they were the wealthy, educated middle class, who came mostly by air. Later, the crowds of refugees included people from all walks of life, including workers. Many of these people came on fishing boats, like this one shown here, arriving in Key West, Florida, in May 1980, part of the last wave of 125,000. (U.P.I.)

Miami, Florida, is the largest Cuban center in the United States with a population of 500,000 Cubans. In 1959, the section of Miami now known as "Little Havana" was rundown. Today it is full of restaurants, nightclubs, and retail businesses that serve the Cuban community and add to the tourist attractions of the city. (Photo of "Little Havana." Courtesy of City of Miami, Office of Information and Visitors.)

Only when it was clear Castro was going to stay in power for a long time did refugees begin to abandon the idea of returning to Cuba. Today many are becoming United States citizens. There are also a small but visible number of extremist Cuban exiles who remain actively anti-Castro. Here an anti-Castro picket waves a Cuban flag during a demonstration near the Cuban Mission to the U.N., where Castro was staying in October 1979 while in New York to address the U.N. General Assembly. (U.P.I.)

Following World War II, thousands of Puerto Ricans came to the United States mainland to take advantage of the employment boom. In 1946 alone, some 40,000 islanders journeyed to New York. The faces of these children on the steps of a Harlem grammar school at lunchtime reflect the Puerto Rican influx. (U.P.I.)

A majority of young Puerto Ricans dropped out of school and turned to menial jobs or, worse than that, to drugs and violence. One of the greatest needs was to help these young people while they were still in school. The efforts of some Puerto Ricans to overcome their own problems and help their countrymen are impressive. Symbolic of these efforts was a silent protest march across the Brooklyn Bridge to the New York City Board of Education sponsored by the National Association for Puerto Rican Civil Rights. The marchers were urging improvement of educational facilities for Puerto Ricans in the city. (U.P.I.)

Most of the post–World War II Puerto Rican immigrants settled in New York City in slums vacated by earlier immigrant groups such as Italians and Jews. The Puerto Ricans came to East Harlem looking for the good life. Instead they found decaying, rat-infested buildings—the only housing they could afford. Here in La Marqueta, the block-long Spanish-American marketplace situated underneath the Penn Central (Amtrak) tracks on upper Park Avenue, Puerto Rican shoppers jam the aisles looking for familiar specialties from home. (U.P.I.)

Other Puerto Ricans are nationalists, working for Puerto Rican independence, a movement in existence since the 1930s. Shown here at a rally in New York in 1980 are former prisoners whose sentences had just been commuted by President Jimmy Carter. From left to right are Rafael Cancel-Miranda, Flores Rodriquez, Lolita Lebron, and Oscar Collazo. Collazo had been sent to jail for allegedly trying to kill President Harry S Truman. The others had sprayed bullets on the floor of the U.S. House of Representatives in 1954, wounding five congressmen. Giving the clenched-fist salute, they vow to continue working for independence. (U.P.I.)

Other protest groups grew from fighting gangs who became social or community groups. In 1970, during the annual Puerto Rican Day Parade down Fifth Avenue in New York, a dramatic moment occurred when a member of the Young Lords, a Puerto Rican group that takes an extreme approach to civil rights for Puerto Ricans, burned a small American flag. (U.P.I.)

Other less radical community groups provide help to improve living conditions all over the United States. The struggle continues, but a new spirit of pride and hope is evident. Here, in a scene repeated in many New York neighborhoods, the domino game moves outdoors, a sign that hot weather has arrived. (U.P.I.)

Chapter 9

Castro Takes Over Cuba

Christopher Columbus discovered Cuba on his first voyage to the New World in 1492. The island was inhabited by the Arawak Indians. Diego de Velázquez and three hundred Spaniards colonized the island in 1511, and in 1522 they imported the first African slaves. During the next two centuries Cuba was a base for Spanish explorers and colonizers of the New World. Extensive cattle farming was developed, along with the growing of sugar cane and other plantation crops.

Harsh Spanish rule led to several Cuban independence movements in the nineteenth century. During the insurrection known as the Ten Years War (1868–1878), slavery was finally abolished. The great Cuban leader José Martí led a new revolt against the Spanish in 1895, cheered on by many North Americans.

Then the United States battleship *Maine* mysteriously blew up in Havana harbor in February 1898. The popular outcry against Spain resulted in the Spanish-American War. It lasted only four months. Spanish rule in the Caribbean was ended, but the United States occupied Cuba until 1902, when the island became independent. However, the United States imposed conditions on the Cubans. These included the right (exercised many times) of the United States to intervene in Cuban affairs "for the protection of life, property, and individual liberty," and to maintain a naval base (Guantánamo) on the island.

The next sixty years were filled with unrest and instability within Cuba under a variety of corrupt governments. At the same time, North Americans came to own a great proportion of the sugar, oil, agriculture, banking, transportation, and other industries. By the 1950s there was a deeply felt need throughout Cuba to replace the dictatorship of Fulgencio Batista. His regime was marked by graft and corruption, torture of dissidents, and misuse of government power.

Long a playland for business people and tourists, Havana seemed to most North Americans a city of plush gambling clubs full of flashing-eyed Latins, gay night life, and endless pleasures for the rich. Most Cubans, however, were extremely poor and illiterate agricultural laborers, who lived in the countryside. Cuba was run by a small, upper-class minority whose interests were tied to those of the United States. Although his years in power were turbulent, Batista could be counted on to defend

American business and political interests, and he stayed in favor with the United States government. As one Cuban said:

> I didn't like Batista and most of my friends didn't like Batista. Because we looked upon him as a dictator. Fidel Castro was looked upon from the people, you know, the middle and upper classes, as someone who was going to bring back democracy to Cuba, and social justice. There was a lot of nationalistic pride involved, from all sides of the political spectrum. Those people from the industrial classes saw Castro as a way to become independent from the North American influence in their businesses. The poorer classes saw Castro as a social form of liberation and getting a better education.[1]

When Fidel Castro succeeded in ousting the Batista government in 1959, he had the backing and the hopes of most of his countrymen. He had promised a revolution that would bring peace and equality to everyone, based on social and economic reforms that would benefit all Cubans. According to one observer at the time:

> The Cuban revolution was really a middle-class revolution, helped economically by the rich people and with the active backing of the middle class.[2]

Another student who had seen the poverty in the rural areas recalled:

I was very much aware that the country needed social reforms in many areas. And as I read materials that Fidel Castro had written, I became more aware that this was an answer for the things that I had seen in the country-side. I saw it also as an answer for the poor people in the city who were experiencing a lot of hardships in terms of everyday living.[3]

The same young Cuban was studying in the United States at the time when Castro marched triumphantly into Havana in January 1959. She spoke of her joy at the event:

All our problems were going to be over then. Finally the revolution had succeeded and things were going to change and we were going to be equal—equality for all people on the island, and everything was going to be peaceful and quiet from now on.[4]

Before the revolution the Cuban population in the United States numbered about fifty thousand. During the last years of the Batista government, Cubans went to the United States at the rate of ten thousand to fifteen thousand annually. These included members of the ruling class who were out of favor as well as those who did not want to live under Batista's rule. There had been an earlier migration in the late nineteenth century of tobacco workers, especially to Tampa, Key West, and New York City, when tobacco plantations were ruined in anti-Spanish rebellions. These cigar makers gave outstanding support to the exiled leader José Martí for the Cuban independence movement.

In 1960, after Castro had been in power for a year or so, the new government made it plain that this was a serious social revolution in which society was to be restructured. A new migration to the United States began. Former Batista supporters, including government officials, policemen, and military men, fled to the United States to avoid imprisonment or death. After summary trials many who stayed were executed for their crimes against the Cuban people.

One of Castro's first acts was the Agrarian Reform Law—under which private landowners were stripped of ownership. He also accepted support from the Cuban Communist Party. In December 1961 he announced that he was a Marxist-Leninist and that the Party must take over the leadership of the revolution. Various elements in Cuban society opposed him. Castro had had to break up a serious counterrevolutionary movement of former landowners and military leaders in the summer of 1959. Confusion and mistakes led to further criticism of the revolution by many who otherwise backed Castro. Others were permanently disaffected, either frightened by the idea of communism or disillusioned by the early years of struggle. In addition, some Cubans felt they could not express their opposition openly:

> People began to be a little more careful to whom they talked and what they said and

when they said it. In other words, there was not much freedom in social intercourse. Already by then there were very strong indications that if you were not pro-government, pro the rebel, you were against them. And people were beginning to be afraid. Also at that time people were beginning to be arrested, cars were being searched for no apparent reason or not very obvious ones. I felt how could we have been so stupid just to take for granted that what Fidel was saying was what he was going to do.[5]

As socialism replaced capitalism, and the government nationalized oil refineries, factories, sugar plantations, banks, and other businesses, major landowners and industrialists left Cuba, for it became clear they would no longer prosper. (Of those who left because their privileges were taken away, Castro said: "They wanted the revolution but not so much.") Many others of the upper-middle class left also. These were managers, military leaders, bank presidents, aristocrats—a whole level of the professional, managerial, entrepreneurial, and commercial classes. Along with them went some ordinary, educated middle-class people who simply didn't trust or approve of the revolution.

Between 1959 and 1962 relations between the United States and Cuba worsened steadily. When its request for a thirty-billion-dollar loan from the United States was turned down, Cuba turned to the Soviet Union for aid in continuing the work of the revolution. As Cuba's Communist ties grew, the United States placed an embargo on the importation of Cuban sugar. Cuba in return nationalized all United States property and intensified its trade with the Soviets. Early in 1961 the United States broke diplomatic relations with Cuba. In April counter-revolutionary Cubans, sponsored and trained by the United States, invaded Cuba at the Bay of Pigs. Within three days Castro's forces had killed or captured the entire invasion group.

Early in 1962 United States President John F. Kennedy placed an almost total embargo on trade between the United States and Cuba, an event which again forced Cuba to turn to Communist countries for economic support now that its chief market was cut off. There was, in addition, a buildup of military assistance and equipment in Cuba by the Soviets. By October it was learned that missile-launching sites were under construction on the island. The United States demanded that the Soviets remove all offensive missiles from Cuba and imposed an air and naval blockade on the island. After four days of tension in which the eyes of the world were trained on Cuba, the Soviets agreed to the removal of the missiles and a reduction in military personnel. The blockade was lifted, although the embargo remained in effect.

Between 1959 and the time of the missile crisis in 1962, when all direct contact with the United States was suspended, 155,000 Cubans had gone to the United States.

Chapter 10

Escape to the United States

The arrival of an unlimited number of Cubans on United States shores was facilitated by the United States attitude of hostility toward Castro. The arriving Cubans were called exiles and were given refugee status.

And at first Castro did not prevent anyone from leaving Cuba. He felt he had no need of people who did not support him wholeheartedly. Indeed, in general he was refusing to allow criticism of his policies in the newspapers or anywhere. He began to demand complete devotion to the revolution.

A former provincial judge explained why he went to the United States.

> As a judge I used to handle only minor offenses, was not involved with the governments, and was independent. But . . . the pressures started to mount to make the judges

political accomplices; they said over the radio that we should go cut cane and teach the illiterates, which I always refused to do. One day a circular arrived from the authorities pressuring us to write "Fatherland or Death" after our signatures and demanding that we give classes in Marxism. That same day I resigned and started to take out papers to come to the United States.[1]

Others in Cuba saw things differently. It was to become the greatest patriotic duty to cut cane each year, and the drive to eradicate illiteracy became perhaps Castro's most successful program. Cuba has one of the lowest rates of illiteracy in any Latin American country today.

Because so many professionals had left Cuba, it was necessary to administer programs, build new homes and hospitals, reorganize land distribution, plant and harvest crops, and feed and clothe the population without their help. Lack of experience and inefficient programs took their toll in the beginning. Many Cubans found the situation intolerable. One former teacher described what happened in her community.

I saw the low-class people taking over. In the town where I was working, a person with no education, with nothing, became the president of the board of education. And that kind of person was leading us and telling us what to do.[2]

Some Cubans were afraid that the government would instill Marxist ideology in their children's minds. A Cuban who left after a term in prison said:

> After my release . . . I was more determined than ever to leave. The main reason now was the children. They were under steady indoctrination. My cellmate in prison had been denounced by his 14-year-old son. If this can happen, the father is no longer a father. He simply breeds for the state.[3]

David Sagarra, a painter, explained why it became impossible for him to continue working in Cuba.

> As a painter I would have had to join the official painters' association in order to obtain paints, brushes, and oils to produce canvasses and paintings. When you eliminate the possibility for an individual to go to the corner and buy a tube of paint, you are really depriving him of freely painting whatever he wants. The government did specify quite clearly that the subject matter was to be limited to whatever did not contradict the revolution.[4]

The Cuban government soon began to place restrictions on the amount of money refugees could take out of the country. As Iraida Gil described it:

> When I came from Cuba I took just three dollars. I was allowed five dollars but I only had three dollars American money. And I took one suitcase for my daughter and me.[5]

Yet Cubans continued to pour into the United States. Many clung to the hope that Castro would be overthrown and that they would be able to return home. The failure of the Bay of Pigs invasion dashed those hopes. Castro tightened security and arrested thousands of citizens. People who were suspected of harboring counterrevolutionaries were held anywhere from a few hours to a few months. A refugee described his experience:

> Having never been involved in politics, living always for work, being respected by everybody, considered always to be a hardworking man and a decent person without political motivations, I was imprisoned on the 17th of April, 1961, and from that time on I was persecuted constantly.[6]

Many Cubans felt that the United States had betrayed them by failing to come to the aid of the invaders at the Bay of Pigs. Nonetheless they still chose to move to the United States. Obtaining permission to leave Cuba became more difficult. Since Castro felt the exiles were running out on a poor country to go to a rich one, he would not let those who left in 1962 take anything of value with them. One refugee remembers:

> I was only able to take out a suit, a pair of shoes, two shirts, a tie, and underwear. Not one penny. My car was taken at the airport. . . . The government gives you a note what you will be allowed to take with you and that was

> all. At that time they were short of everything. They could use everything that you left behind.[7]

Working-class people were beginning to leave Cuba also. Like the wealthy and middle classes, some of them felt that Castro had betrayed their cause also.

> We had been promised a government controlled *by* the people. . . . We got a government committed to absolute control *of* the people. I had to get out. This is not easy. It means you are leaving the country you love, the country where you were raised.[8]

A fisherman who left for the United States said:

> If *El Caballo* (Fidel) tried to help us, then he failed. He failed because his ideas didn't work out; but he couldn't admit it and kept the idea all the same.[9]

When commercial airline traffic was canceled at the time of the missile crisis, Cubans who wanted to leave had to find other ways of getting to the United States. Some endured dangerous journeys to Florida, ninety miles away, on rafts or in small boats. Others flew to third countries, such as Spain or Mexico, and then went on to the United States. A few hundred came on North American ships which had been sent to Cuba with medical supplies exchanged in prisoner release programs.

Escape by sea was the most dangerous of all

because the coast was patrolled by Cuban planes and gunboats. One man, Rafael, devised a plan to commandeer one of the boats that regularly ran up and down the coast. He chose a group of people who came from all walks of life to join him. With meticulous planning Rafael and his group—which mushroomed to eight-five—eventually made it to Florida.

The ban on flights between Cuba and the United States lasted three years. Then in September 1965 Castro and the United States came to an agreement for a special airlift program under which some four thousand Cubans a month were flown to Miami. Priority was given to close relatives of refugees already in the United States. Distant relatives and some other Cubans followed.

Cubans who wanted to leave had to register with the Cuban government. Cubans already in America who wanted to get friends and relatives out of Cuba also sent requests to Castro through the United States government. Not all the requests were granted, but by the time the "aerial bridge" was shut down in 1973, some 260,000 refugees had been airlifted to the United States.

Castro's reasons for allowing the "freedom flights" are not certain. Some people have speculated that he wanted to export the elderly and others who were unable to work, and that he wanted to get rid of those who spoke and worked against his government. Several years earlier Castro himself had spoken of his desire to rid himself of "parasites":

If some more want to go to Miami, let them
go to Miami! Each time that a boatload of
parasites leaves—whether for Spain or for
Miami—the Republic comes out ahead. What
do you lose, working men and women? . . .
What do you lose when a parasite leaves? One
less beefsteak eater, one less driver of a fancy
car, one drinker less . . . and if he has a good
apartment, that apartment will go to a working
family that has a lot of children.[10]

Still, Castro would not permit certain people to
leave Cuba, including draft-age men and people in
vital occupations. Some in these classifications
decided to leave by illegal means. One exile recalled
how eighty-eight Cubans escaped by truck to the
American naval base at Guantánamo Bay on Cuba's
southeastern shore:

Everyone piled out and began running for the
fence about 200 yards away. One of our men
began shooting at the guards to hold them off,
and they answered the fire while we were
climbing over the barbed wire fences, shred-
ding our hands. We threw the children over.[11]

Many who preferred to be airlifted out were hesi-
tant about applying, because the consequences could
be severe. Very often the airlift applicants lost their
jobs and had to wait months or even years to get
out of Cuba. Many had to work without pay
harvesting sugar and doing other agricultural jobs
while waiting to be processed.

Armando, a young Cuban who was about to be drafted, chose a dangerous alternative—he stowed away in the wheel well of a jet plane bound for Madrid. Frozen stiff, but still alive, Armando landed later in Madrid. From there he took a flight —with a seat this time—to the United States.

From time to time Castro has allowed certain groups to leave Cuba, usually when relations between Cuba and the United States were showing signs of improvement. In 1978, for example, he agreed to release three thousand political prisoners, some of whom had been kept in jail since the overthrow of Batista in 1959.

One of the prisoners was Frank Emmick, an American businessman who had been held on spying charges since 1963. He was released in 1978 after the intervention of three United States congressmen. Later he described the treatment of political prisoners:

> I was . . . placed into a completely dark refrigerated room, stripped down to my underclothes and forced to sleep uncovered on the floor for eight days. It was so dark that I couldn't see my hands in front of me, and I could move about only by using the walls as my guide.[12]

For a time Emmick was kept in an underground dungeon:

> . . . approximately 650 political prisoners were jammed like sardines, forced to sleep on an old, poorly cemented floor, with little ventila-

tion and where the sun, moon or the stars could never be seen.[13]

That thousands of political prisoners managed to survive such conditions for years was due, says Emmick, to their determination to resist communism.

In spring 1980, after quarreling for some time with several Latin American countries about the question of asylum for Cuban refugees, Castro suddenly withdrew his guards from the front entrance to the Peruvian embassy in Havana. The embassy opened its unguarded gates, and 10,000 Cubans rushed in seeking political asylum on the grounds. Castro again allowed the exodus of refugees that followed. It is not clear yet to what extent the existence of poor economic conditions in Cuba provided the reasons behind this exodus. In any event, the United States, which also offered political asylum to the Cubans, was not fully prepared for the number of people who left, and many of the 125,000 who arrived in the United States were still in processing centers awaiting placement at the end of the year.

In all, some 600,000 Cubans have come to the United States since 1959. The story of how they have adapted to American life is unusual in the history of immigration. This is partly because of the character of the Cuban refugees, and partly because of American attitudes toward them. But the story of the refugees is also inextricably tied to the Castro revolution. This revolution, so unlike previous revolutions in Latin America where one oppressor simply replaced another, leaving the structure of society completely unchanged, has profoundly shaken the Western Hemisphere. In its short history, the revolution has won fervent support from many people—both on the left and the right—and gained an equal amount of criticism and opposition.

Fidel Castro remains one of the most charismatic leaders of any society today. Though some United States analysts would disagree, Castro's entrance into the Soviet bloc now seems less a planned, inevitable step than a result of United States intransigence and its desire to isolate Cuba early on. The fact that progress under communism has been difficult and sometimes stormy can be laid to the vicissitudes of building a new society as well as to ideological struggles. Whether Cuba is better off today than it was twenty years ago is a question that cannot be answered in absolute terms.

Only the future will show if the restructured country and its citizens can survive the pressures of uncertain economic conditions and of the larger political battle between East and West in order to fulfill the original dreams of the revolution. Until the future is with us, we cannot know whether yet another outpouring of people from Cuba will be on the way to the United States, where a new Cuban home away from home is already changing the patterns of American life there.

Chapter 11

Miami: A Home Away from Home

In the first wave of immigrants from Castro's Cuba were many who had been educated in the United States and knew the language and the country. They brought not only their Cuban identity, values, and customs but also their managerial skills, executive experience, and higher education.

They adapted easily to life in the United States. Those who had worked for North American firms in Cuba were shifted to high-level positions in the United States. Few had any problems finding employment. As one refugee put it, "The men that came in 1960 were the cream of the crop."

In addition to those who transferred within companies, there were also immigrants who had funds to set up businesses in the United States. Manuel Fernandez, for example, whose ten-million-dollar slaughterhouse was taken over by the Cuban government, managed to save a part of his fortune. This he used to establish a successful bakery business in Miami. Similarly, David Egozi and Eugene Ramos, who left Cuba in 1960 after the government seized their shoe firm, smuggled out forty thousand dollars with them. With this and a thirty-five-thousand-dollar loan, they established a shoe business in Miami which, by 1971, had earnings of $2.6 million.

More remarkable are the success stories of Cubans who lost everything in Cuba and who came to America virtually penniless. Carlos Arboleya, for example, had been a banker in Cuba until October 1960, when Castro nationalized the banks. Arboleya had only forty dollars when he arrived in Miami, Florida. After failing to find another banking job—"No one wanted a Cuban with ten years' banking experience"—he took a forty-five-dollar-a-week job as inventory clerk in a shoe factory. Within eighteen months Arboleya worked his way up to become chief accounting officer at the factory.

Although there are similar rags-to-riches stories, not everyone was able to make it without help. For one thing, hundreds of thousands of Cuban refugees were pouring into the United States, and there were not enough jobs. For another, most of the refugees entered this country through Miami, looking for jobs and homes, glutting that city with people. Soon the residents of Miami began to see the Cubans as an economic burden.

When agencies ran out of funds to help the refugees, the federal government assumed the responsibility. President Dwight Eisenhower made one million dollars available to set up the Cuban

Refugee Emergency Center in Miami. This was followed in 1961 by the Cuban Refugee Program, sponsored by President Kennedy, who said:

> I hope these measures will be understood as an immediate expression of the firm desire of the people of the United States to be of tangible assistance to refugees until such time as better circumstances enable them to return to their permanent homes in health, in confidence, and with unimpaired pride.[1]

Needy Cubans were provided with food, financial aid, and health services. Many also received free vocational and English instruction. In addition, low-interest, long-term loans were made available for students to go to colleges, graduate schools, and professional schools, as well as for professional people to take refresher and supplementary courses. But the primary purpose of the program was to re-settle the refugees in parts of the United States other than Miami.

In addition to government agencies, several voluntary organizations helped to relocate refugees. It sometimes took as many as fifty volunteers to resettle one refugee. As a result of the resettlement program, Cuban communities developed in many states, especially New York, New Jersey, California, and Illinois.

In 1976 a federal task force recommended that the refugee program be phased out within five years. By that time only 5,000 people were still in need of help and that number was expected to drop.

Altogether, between 1961 and 1976, $1.1 billion was spent on assisting more than 600,000 Cuban refugees to settle in the United States. During 1972 the peak year of the program, 90,000 people were given financial assistance.

Those who were most in need of help were the women and children who came to the United States alone and the elderly who were too old or too sick to earn a living. Many had been wealthy in Cuba. Adapting to their poorer circumstances in the United States was extremely difficult. Middle-class Cubans had been used to having maids to do the cooking and cleaning. As a result, many refugee women were not prepared for their life in America. One middle-class Cuban woman who was asked her opinion of the United States simply said, "I hate it."[2]

The move to the United States was particularly hard for children who came here without their parents. During the early years of Castro's regime a number of Cubans, unable to get out of the country, decided to send their children to the United States so that they, at least, would be safe. For the children, arriving in a strange country where they knew no one and did not speak the language was often a traumatic experience.

The children were first sent to camps near Miami, and then they were resettled in orphanages or foster homes, sometimes as far away as Colorado. Cuban parents who feared that their children were going to be taken away by the Communists lost them in another way.

The majority of the unaccompanied children

arrived between 1960 and 1962. Most of them were reunited with their parents after the freedom flights started in 1965. As one young Cuban immigrant said, "To us, the family means everything!"[3]

Most Cubans, who arrived in Miami, wanted to stay there. With its large Spanish-speaking population, its warm climate, its Cuban restaurants and stores, Miami seemed like a home away from home. A worker on the refugee program said:

> It takes extraordinary courage for a Cuban to leave relatives and friends in Miami to go to an unfamiliar world with a climate in sharp contrast to Cuba's and Florida's. It takes remarkable qualities of heart and mind for, say, the dean of an ancient university, the senior judge of a national court, the chief executive of a large industrial plant, persons no longer young, to go back to school to become teachers and librarians. This is nevertheless what many prominent Cuban exiles are doing.[4]

One man who endured the upheaval of resettlement was Dr. Rigoberto Areces. Forced to leave behind a six-million-dollar fortune in Cuba, Areces was relocated in Iowa where the temperature often goes below zero. After having been president of his own bank in Cuba, he was obliged to take a job as a bank employee in Iowa. However, putting his expertise to use, within six years he had been promoted to bank manager.

Dr. Areces chose to stay in Iowa, but many Cubans who had been resettled throughout the

United States eventually returned to Miami with enough money to lead a comfortable life. One immigrant explained why Miami, with its two languages and two cultures, was so attractive:

> I want to move back to Miami so my children will know they are Cuban as well as American. I didn't want my children to forget Spanish the way immigrant children in America have always forgotten to combine the two ways of life so that neither one will be lost. Maybe I'm optimistic but most Cubans are. How could we be otherwise, when we look back at how far we have come in this country.[5]

Iraida Itturalde put forth her idea of the Cuban experience in the United States. Her family hasn't "hit it off that well," first in Miami and then in New Jersey. She arrived in the United States as a young girl in 1962.

> I think Americans were really surprised that the Cubans in ten years are well off. I think the political immigration is part of the cause for the economic success of the Cubans in this country and I'm saying the ones who came first. But most of the Cubans . . . that have come in the economic migration are following the same patterns as the Italians, the Irish. They are taking longer to hit it off because they're not professionals, they don't have the means that the first Cubans had in their country before. Now they realize that the Cuban success story

is a myth, but it wasn't a myth in the beginning. It's a myth in the over all. There are a lot of lower-class Cubans that have come and are working in factories. Most of the peasants are working in factories. The ones that owned little shops are owning little shops lining the avenue when you go by. The Chinese-Cubans have their restaurants here or their laundries, the same thing they had there, you know, but they don't work in banks, that type of thing.[6]

In one section of Miami, now known as "Little Havana," Cubans have re-created the atmosphere and customs of the country they left behind. In 1959 this section of Miami was a run-down neighborhood. Today it is full of restaurants, nightclubs, and retail businesses that serve the Cuban community and add to the tourist attractions of Miami.

An article in *The New York Times* sums up what Miami is today:

> In the 1950s Greater Miami was basically provincial and rather somnolent, like many Southern towns, but it changed mainly as a result of the Cuban influx, into a bustling internationally oriented city, the nation's only truly bilingual and bicultural metropolitan area. Of its 1.65 million people today, about 650,000 are Hispanic Americans, and more than 500,000 of them are Cubans. Demographers predicted before the present Cuban influx that well before the 21st century, Greater

Miami will become the largest urban area in the United States with a Hispanic majority.

Also, thousands of Latin Americans and Spaniards, many of them wealthy, have settled here in the last few years, opening businesses, investing in real estate and stimulating commercial ties with their countries. Over the years, Cuban Americans have provided the managerial and highly trained clerical base for this new direction of Miami's economic activity, resulting in an urbane and sophisticated character that this area never had when it was only a seasonal tourist destination.[7]

At the present time the Cuban population in Miami is overrepresented by whites, a result of the relationship between class and race in prerevolutionary Cuba. However, it is probably also true that fewer blacks came to the United States from Cuba, owing to their understanding that race relations in the United States are less happy than they are in socialist Cuba. The blacks who did come live mainly in the northeastern United States and indeed suffer both ethnic and racial discrimination.

The success and the predominance of Spanish-speaking people in Miami have caused resentment among some Anglos. They began to feel that they were victims of reverse discrimination—many jobs required employees to speak Spanish. Frank Soler, editor of the Spanish-language *El Miami Herald,* noted that

> . . . in some cases, Cubans themselves become obnoxious. A minority began saying, "This is a Cuban town. We run this place."[8]

Over the years Cuban attitudes toward the United States have changed. When they first came here, most refugees expected their stay to be temporary —until Castro was overthrown. They tended, therefore, to stay in Cuban communities, keeping their language and traditions in the hope of returning to Cuba one day. Very few looked upon the United States as a permanent home. In the twelve years from 1961 to 1973 only forty-three thousand Cubans became United States citizens.

Only when it was clear that Castro was going to be in power for a long time did Cuban refugees begin to abandon thoughts of returning to Cuba. In 1976, forty thousand Cubans in Miami became citizens of the United States. The refugees were developing a new feeling about their adopted country.

In addition to joining the North American mainstream as citizens, Cuban-Americans have also been showing a greater interest in United States politics. More Cuban-Americans have registered to vote; more have run for office themselves. Cuban-born Alfredo Duran, who was elected state chairman of the Democratic party in Florida in 1976, said:

> There was a time when becoming an American citizen was regarded by some older leaders as unpatriotic. Now, everybody wants to have an

American passport and the right to vote. The
refugees have at least realized that there is no
way to turn the clock back. Possibly, this is
our way of celebrating the Bicentennial.[9]

On the other hand, there is a small but visible
number of extremist Cuban exiles who remain
actively anti-Castro. They feel the United States
government betrayed their desire to overthrow
Castro. Their acts of terrorism are reported repeatedly in the newspapers. But whether they reflect
the desire of many of the Cuban immigrants to
return to Cuba if the situation there should change
is not known. Undoubtedly some would, but many
others and their children regard their move as
permanent. A doctor's wife, who had to make a
completely new life for herself in the United States,
said:

When your world turns upside down you don't
have money or your family to rely on, but
only yourself. I never thought I would get over
losing my country, my place in society then,
but now I must admit that I would not like to
start over a third time. To go back to the old
life would be impossible, because we are
different people.[10]

Cuban immigrants to the United States have had
many different experiences, yet personal accounts
reveal one common attitude toward their new
country. The wealthy as well as those of more

modest means speak alike of the most cherished aspect of life in the United States. David Sagarra said:

> By coming here I did gain something that I perhaps could summarize in very few words. . . . It's freedom in many levels of human endeavor.[11]

And Iraida Gil, who at one point had to work as a dollar-an-hour garment worker, declared:

> When I came here from my country I was living in New Jersey. . . . Very cold apartment, eight windows with no heat. . . . Then the winter came—no blankets, no coal, nothing. It doesn't matter. . . . I was so happy to be here. The most important thing we were looking for was freedom. When you lose it once, you really know what freedom is.[12]

FROM
PUERTO RICO

Chapter 12

Puerto Ricans: Citizen Migrants

Before the Spanish-American War of 1898, Puerto Rico, like Cuba, was a Spanish colony. Although it was not directly involved in the war, Puerto Rico was handed over to the United States "as compensation for the losses and expenses" of the war.

The Puerto Ricans, who had long disliked Spanish domination, equally opposed United States rule. Following a brief period of military occupation, the United States granted the island a degree of self-government. The Puerto Ricans pressured for independence. In 1917 the United States unilaterally gave Puerto Ricans United States citizenship, an act that was widely resented by the Puerto Ricans. In 1946 the United States appointed the first native-born governor of the island, and in 1948 the governorship became an elective office. In 1952 a Puerto Rican constitution was approved by the United States and accepted by a Puerto Rican referendum. It provided for commonwealth status for the island, which remains a United States possession. Its inhabitants are subject to United States federal laws, including military conscription. However, Puerto Ricans on the island cannot vote in United States elections. They have no representation in Congress aside from an elected commissioner who has no vote. Puerto Ricans pay no federal taxes. As citizens, they are free to travel to and from "the mainland" with no restrictions other than the price of a ticket.

For most Puerto Ricans life has been hard. Overpopulation, unemployment, and poverty have always prevailed. The island's economy improved greatly in the twentieth century, but it was mainly the United States investors who reaped large profits from their interests in land, sugar and tobacco production, and industry, especially in the growing tourist trade. These activities provided some employment for Puerto Ricans, but wages were perennially low. Many could find no work at all. Nonetheless, the income of most persons increased greatly after World War II to become the highest in Latin America.

Beginning in the early 1900s, Puerto Ricans began to make their way to the mainland. Until the introduction of air travel in the 1940s, they went by ship. Tickets were expensive, costing as much as many Puerto Ricans made in a year. To avoid the expense, some stowed away on freighters coming north. Stowaways who were caught generally had to work for their passage. One young man was brought to the ship's cook:

There I was introduced to the tallest mountain of pots, pans, and cauldrons I had ever seen in my life. The general idea was that I was supposed to keep them shiny as a new Lincoln copper penny all through the voyage.

Besides these kitchen chores, the other tasks of an average stowaway was to mop the floors, shine brass,—and do anything that anybody aboard ship thought he might place upon your shoulders to lighten his particular daily responsibilities. And don't you dare protest![1]

By 1920 some eleven thousand Puerto Ricans had made their way to the United States. The majority settled in New York City, where they felt sure they would find good jobs and wages. Most were disappointed. With few skills to offer and little knowledge of English, they usually ended up taking menial, unskilled jobs which paid barely enough to live on. One Puerto Rican recalled that the only way he and his brother managed to get by in New York was by working different shifts and sharing their working clothes:

But the fact remained that we only had one pair of working pants between the two of us. And that was a fact for months, until the day when we were not too tired after one of us came from work, to go out and buy one pair of pants. By that I really mean, until we could spare the few dollars—the cost of a pair of good working pants—without disturbing the very delicate balance between what we earned and what we had to spend on room, food, and other incidentals.[2]

Adjusting to a new way of life in a strange country was difficult, especially for the early groups, because they were pioneers—leading the way for the masses who were to come later. Each new arrival had to learn to fend for himself quickly. Celia Vice came to New York before the Great Depression and was one of the first Puerto Rican women to obtain a real estate and insurance broker's license. She described the typical experience of the Puerto Rican who arrived at that time:

> . . . [he] had immediately to try to forget his Island and begin to learn English because there were few Spanish-speaking people in the city at that time. He had to take whatever job was available in order to survive, and with this, become accustomed to a completely new life, with no warm breezes, no beautiful and clean sandy beaches around him. . . .[3]

In fact, what most Puerto Ricans had left behind was not nearly as appealing as "beautiful and clean sandy beaches." Conditions there were often deplorable. The poor lived in huts or shacks made of packing boxes and tarpaper. An average family of seven lived in one or two rooms on a diet of cornmeal mush, rice, and beans. Puerto Rico in the early twentieth century was, as one observer put it:

> . . . the sinkhole of the Caribbean, with a life expectancy of 32, a place where the American

rulers would sit around the palaces . . . while *jíbaros* [rural people] died in the mountains from . . . parasites.[4]

Because the island was economically dependent on the United States, the Great Depression of the 1930s severely affected Puerto Rico. Wages fell— in some cases to as little as ten cents an hour—and unemployment increased. Puerto Ricans, believing that conditions must surely be better on the mainland, continued to come to the United States. As the daughter of one migrant family explained:

> When we came to New York the country was in the midst of a depression and if things were bad on the mainland, they were worse in Puerto Rico.[5]

That family was luckier than some. The mother managed to find work that paid twice what she could have earned in Puerto Rico. But that didn't mean that life was easy for the family:

> It was a miserable menial job, but with the $12.40 a week she earned for six days, eight hours a day, and sometimes half a day on Sundays, she was able to keep her family together. . . . [She was] afraid . . . of losing her job, getting sick, of many other fears.[6]

She was earning at just about the minimum wage level of twenty-five cents an hour, established in 1938.

Yet Puerto Ricans continued to come to the

United States, believing that this was the land of opportunity, that they would make their fortune. When World War II broke out and people were needed to work in defense factories, Puerto Ricans were encouraged to come to the United States. (They also, of course, served in the armed forces.) Some traveled on military transport ships, which were used when enemy blockades made travel between Puerto Rico and the mainland difficult.

After the war, jobs continued to be plentiful and thousands of Puerto Ricans came to the United States to take advantage of the employment boom. By this time ship travel had given way to air travel and, at eighty dollars, the airplane fare was much cheaper than the boat fare. Still, there were many Puerto Ricans who could not afford such a sum. Some managed to borrow the money; some bought their tickets on credit; and some took cheap charter flights.

The charter flights, which flourished in the early days of post–World War II migration, were in many cases organized by swindlers. Posing as recruiters, they lured Puerto Ricans aboard their flights with promises of a job in New York. They charged thirty-five dollars for the flight, plus a fee for their services. Puerto Ricans who arrived in New York often found that the promised jobs did not exist. Some people never even arrived:

> The hustlers moved in with the charter flights
> and created a kind of airborne steerage, with
> shaking aircraft, packed with women and

> screaming children, skimming out over the
> Atlantic, pushing against the headwinds of
> the North, moving on, leaving it all behind,
> heading for New York. A lot of the planes
> never made it, falling into the sea with their
> cargoes of people. . . .[7]

The hustlers did not stay in business for long. The
law soon stepped in to put an end to their fraudulent
practices and unsafe flights.

The mass migration of Puerto Ricans to the
mainland continued. In 1946 alone, some forty
thousand islanders journeyed to New York—an
increase of 200 percent over the year before. Most
came on one of the many commercial flights between San Juan and New York City. The trip took
anywhere from eight hours to fourteen hours—
quick compared with the ship voyage but by no
means painless. Some of the flights were definitely
"no frills." The late-night Thrift Flight—run
primarily for Puerto Rican passengers—was particularly unpleasant because the cabins were not
pressurized, and the plane could not fly above
storms. The sudden dips during a storm played
havoc with the passengers' stomachs.

Despite the bumpy trip the migrants looked to
the United States, and New York in particular, with
hope and anticipation. Some were not disappointed
by what they found. Herman Badillo came from
Puerto Rico in 1941 as an orphan. He went on to
become a United States congressman from New
York. He said:

I thought I had come into Paradise. I had been starving for seven years and now I got three meals and could eat my fill. I had a pair of shoes. What made the greatest impression on me was that people did not seem to be hungry and instead of the widespread unemployment I saw all around me in Puerto Rico, most people seemed to have work. This alone was enough to impress me.[8]

But for others New York was a nightmare. Those who arrived in the winter were shocked by the cold. Coming from a warm climate, they had only summer clothes, and most could not afford to buy winter coats.

The Puerto Rican Community Development Project, a New York City community agency, reported:

They arrive in the glittering city anticipating opportunities for security and advancement. They are white, black and all shades in between. They often carry with them the name of a friend or a relative who will assist them with lodging and who will aid them in their search for employment. They journey over 1600 miles of ocean to melt into the life of the city and in many cases become a part of its statistics on poverty.[9]

Still they came, in the hope that their fates would be better than those of most. The Puerto Rican

Forum, another community agency, noted that "despite the fact that some of the stories are . . . of defeat, each newcomer feels that for him it will be different."[10]

Chapter 13

From Tarpaper Shacks to Rat-Infested Tenements

Poverty, prejudice, low wages, a foreign culture and language—these are not what dreams are made of. But these were the realities that the majority of Puerto Ricans faced when they reached the United States.

One of the first of these realities was discrimination based on color. Puerto Ricans recognized their heritage of racial intermingling—white, black, and Indian. At home on the island they tended to accept as equal people of any color, though whites certainly were predominant in the upper classes. However, when they arrived in the United States, they found that color decided where you lived, whether you got a job, and who your friends were. The writer Piri Thomas, a dark-skinned Puerto Rican, was turned down for a selling job because the "designated territory is fully capacitated"; his Puerto Rican friend Louie was hired. Mr. Thomas wrote:

. . . Louie and I knew what was shakin' at the same . . . time. The difference between me and Louie was he was white.[1]

In spite of United States rule on the island, Puerto Ricans were poor and uneducated. They were coming to the United States to lift themselves out of poverty, and new arrivals often had to take any job they could get. Many migrants, especially women, took jobs in the garment industry. The work in the garment shops was hard, the wages were low, and working conditions were often unsafe:

One place I was in at 107th Street, you didn't have any fire escape and the building was a wreck. If it ever caught fire we'd have all been gone. Once I know the fire inspector came around and he said to the manager, "What have you been doing, slipping some dollars to the firemen around here?" He said the boiler in the building was held together by a hairpin.[2]

Most workers were paid according to the number of pieces they finished, so each workday was an exhausting race.

Even when they found jobs, the Puerto Ricans were not free of worry. Many faced discrimination from fellow workers. They were the last to be hired and the first to be fired or laid off. Often a husband would send for his wife and children in Puerto Rico on the strength of a job he had landed. But by the time they arrived, he would be out of work again. Juan Antonio López brought his family over after getting an eighty-dollar-a-week job as a construction worker in New York. In Puerto Rico he had earned sixteen dollars a week as a sugar-cane cutter. López was laid off repeatedly, so conditions were not much better than they had been in his home village. Despite their hardships the López family hoped things would get better.

But for many Puerto Ricans racial prejudice and low incomes locked them into living conditions that were substandard. Most of the post–World War II migrants settled in New York City in slums vacated by earlier immigrant groups such as the Italians and the Jews. Into the East Harlem area of New York the Puerto Ricans came looking for the good life. Instead they found decaying, rat-infested buildings —the only housing they could afford. Often entire families would live in two small rooms:

> A bathtub may be located in the kitchen-dining room, which may also be a passage to the rest of the apartment. The enamel lid covering the tub is frequently the utility table. Some rooms have no windows or any other source of ventilation and are almost as dark in the day time as at night. The rooms of these apartments are generally so small that they seem overcrowded with only a few pieces of furniture in them.[3]

Conditions were slightly better in the more modern apartments—but not much. But those Puerto Ricans who could afford to move to a better neighborhood often found themselves isolated, considered to be different. One young Puerto Rican remembered:

> When we first came here we lived in a good neighborhood and were the only Puerto Ricans. Everyone else was Jewish, and it was hard for me to go to school. I had a lot of troubles and problems and I didn't speak the language. I didn't have any friends. I had no clothes and had to wear the same thing all the time. There were three kids in the family and we didn't have enough money.[4]

Some Puerto Ricans decided to try their luck in other locations. They moved to the industrial and farming areas of New Jersey, or to Chicago, Boston, or other large cities. Few fared any better there than they had in New York.

Many Puerto Ricans in New York and elsewhere who were trapped in slum housing hoped that public housing would solve their problems. High-rise housing projects for low-income families were built by the government to replace slums being torn down as part of urban renewal. Not everyone could be accommodated in the new projects, however, and those who could sometimes faced a long wait.

The housing projects had their own problems. Many were vertical cities in which crime was common. People were afraid to leave their apartments. A sixth-grade Puerto Rican suggested:

> . . . take these people and move them into the project. In the projects they have more respect

> than they do for the old buildings. And the
> policemen watch the buildings. You know,
> there's more space. It's fire proof. And they
> have better supplies. . . . My mother don't like
> them because there's been too many killed.
> The elevators get stuck.[5]

Many Puerto Ricans were willing to put up with
low-paying jobs and poor housing so that their
children could get a good education in the United
States. However, schooling was the endeavor in
which Puerto Ricans were most severely discriminated against. The migrant students were thrown
into a system that ignored the fact that they couldn't
speak English. They were expected to "pick it up."
When the assistant principal in one East Harlem
school was asked what the children who didn't speak
English were supposed to do, he replied:

> They just have to wait till they pick it up—
> and in the meantime, if there is something
> urgent to tell the child, the teacher gets one
> of the other children to translate. There are
> always children in the class who can speak
> both Spanish and English.[6]

Even when teachers could speak Spanish, they
were not permitted to do so in the classroom in the
hope that students would "pick up" English. When,
through no fault of their own, the children couldn't
understand what was being said to them, they were
often considered to be retarded or slow learners.

One Puerto Rican who went to United States schools during the 1950s spoke of his frustration:

> My teacher and I could not communicate with each other because each spoke a different language and neither one spoke the language of the other. This made *me* stupid, or retarded, or at least disadvantaged.[7]

By the time he learned English, he was so far behind the other students that he never caught up: "It was like swimming with lead bracelets." Twenty years later a student reported a similar situation to the United States Commission on Civil Rights:

> I feel that the teachers don't care about the students. . . . A Spanish-speaking student comes into the room. Immediately that person is considered dumb without even being given a chance.[8]

Another student recalled that Puerto Rican students were given no encouragement to reach their goals:

> There is discrimination against Puerto Rican students, but it comes out in a very sly way. Being Puerto Rican, I was put in the worst classes. The guidance counselor was very negative about the whole thing. . . . my brother . . . wanted to go to medical school, but they said no because they thought he wouldn't make it. Now my brother is a bac-

teriologist. He went to a college in the Bronx and he still studies. I think my brother could have been a doctor.[9]

A teacher in East Harlem said:

What's the use of worrying about these kids? Between their lousy way of living and their Spanish, we're lost before we begin. . . .

Do you really think for one minute that these kids will ever amount to anything? In ten years you'll be unable to recognize New York because there will be so many Puerto Ricans here.[10]

Discrimination in housing and employment— against these overwhelming odds, what chance did the Puerto Ricans stand of improving their lot? Some felt there was no chance at all, that there was no point in even trying to succeed. But others were aware of their rights and of the achievements of earlier immigrant groups who had suffered similar hardships. They were determined to fight.

Chapter 14

The Struggle Continues

The poverty and prejudice that Puerto Ricans faced in New York and other cities had harmful effects. For some it was too much to be stopped at every turn, to be described in a New York City newspaper as "poverty-numbed, naive natives. . . . weaklings . . . unable physically, mentally or financially to compete. . . ."

Many Puerto Ricans who could not find jobs, or keep jobs, or earn enough to live on, resorted to welfare—sometimes for years. Carmen Santana, for instance, turned to welfare when she found that she could not earn enough to pay a baby-sitter to look after her children. Fourteen years later she was still living on welfare, and she could see little point in looking for work.

A similar sense of defeat gripped young Puerto Ricans who were having a hard time at school. Unable to keep up with their schoolwork, the majority—80 percent in 1978 in New York City—

dropped out and turned to menial jobs or, worse than that, to drugs and violence. As Herman Badillo pointed out:

> We have plenty of jobs in the skyscrapers of midtown Manhattan; the problem is that kids can't spell.[1]

Some young people sold drugs because they felt they could succeed there where they failed in school. A young man from New York's Lower East Side said:

> A lot of kids want an education to get out of here. But in order to survive, they're dealing [selling drugs]. Kids ten and eleven make more money than their old man in the factory.[2]

Others took drugs to blot out reality; addiction was high among young Puerto Ricans. Some reached the point where all they cared about was getting more of "the white powder," heroin.

> The cheapest "bag" or packet of the white powder costs $3; many addicts need from three to 10 "bags" a day to stay high, or they sicken and become maddened by the pain and craving. To support the habit, many will steal (from their own and other homes) or shoplift. . . .[3]

Drug addiction and crime were often associated with fighting gangs. During the 1950s and 1960s in particular, many young Puerto Ricans joined gangs, thinking that this would gain them acceptance as

North Americans. Gang warfare was common all over the city among young people of many ethnic backgrounds.

For some Puerto Ricans welfare, crime, and drug addiction became a way of life. In 1978, 34 percent of all Puerto Ricans in New York City were on welfare; the other 66 percent found a way to get by on their own. From the very beginning of the mass migration many Puerto Ricans refused to sign up for welfare because of their pride—even when their earnings were so low that they were eligible. When a welfare worker told one woman that she qualified for welfare payments, she replied:

> Forget it. . . . As long as I can work to support my children, I don't want *welfare*. Not the way they treat you.[4]

The urgency that many newcomers felt as they searched for a job and home was eased if they could call on a relative or friend to help. Eduardo Garcia, who went from San Juan to New York in 1952, helped his in-laws get settled in their new home with a loan and refused to accept repayment because

> It's family. Something that we do because we are happy if we are in good condition. That's more than money—to have the happiness in the family.[5]

But not every newcomer was lucky enough to have the support of family and friends. In some cases there was even antagonism between newcomers and other Puerto Ricans who were already settled in the United States. One recent arrival complained:

> Instead of offering a hand, the ones that come first try to keep the others down. If a veteran [Puerto Rican] is working as a salesman, he goes from door to door to exploit his compatriots rather than going to the houses of Americans who have the money. Here we Hispanos are after each other's necks so we have to be on our guard.
>
> The trouble with the Puerto Ricans in New York is that each lives for himself and they're all scared to death.[6]

Some Puerto Ricans did manage to leave poverty behind them. Nick Lugo, for instance, started off as a dishwasher. In ten years he became owner of a real estate agency and travel bureau which earned him one million dollars the first year. Cayetano Vallejo learned a new trade when he came to the United States and, after saving and borrowing, opened a factory in Chicago. He had to take many chances, financial and otherwise, but his efforts paid off and his business was a success.

Equally impressive, on a different level, have been the efforts of some Puerto Ricans to overcome their own problems, and then to help their fellow countrymen. Eulogio Cedeño, for example, had all the signs of being a loser who would be swallowed up by Spanish Harlem. A former gang member and ex-convict, Cedeño decided to pick himself up. First he kicked the drug habit. Then he reorganized his fighting gang into a community service group whose members restored abandoned buildings in their deteriorating neighborhood.

Many other fighting gangs became social or community groups, especially as the members got older. The community groups were often helped by other concerned Puerto Ricans who provided moral and financial help. The East Harlem Protestant Parish was particularly active, offering practical help to drug addicts and the unemployed. An off-shoot of the parish was the Neighborhood Narcotics Committee. It was conceived by a Puerto Rican who was shocked by the horrible effects of drugs on his friends and neighbors.

One of the greatest needs was to help young Puerto Ricans while they were still in school, and to prevent them from dropping out and turning to drugs. One woman who worked hard to achieve this was Awilda Orta. She was a Puerto Rican principal of a New York City intermediate school that stressed bilingual education.

Orta believed that teaching Puerto Rican students about their culture was essential to building a good self-image. José Cruz, a teacher in the same school, also felt that the children would work better with a person of their own background. If the principal and teachers didn't speak Spanish, the students and their parents felt alienated. But that school was unusual. Despite government recognition of the need for bilingual education many schools have not adopted it. In 1978 it was estimated that only about twenty-five hundred of the more than forty-five thousand teachers in the New York City school system were Hispanic. An adviser on Puerto Rican affairs noted that:

> The average Puerto Rican in the average city school is still doing the Dick and Jane thing— and that has no relation to Pablo and José.[7]

The situation has started to improve. More and more Puerto Ricans have realized that they can have a voice in what happens in their community. Young Puerto Ricans in particular have started to become more politically aware, advocating that Puerto Ricans "wake up . . . defend what's yours." Those who are fighting for the rights of Puerto Ricans range from civic groups to the Young Lords, a revolutionary group that takes an extreme approach to getting those rights. The Young Lords' program states that:

> We are opposed to violence—the violence of hungry children, illiterate adults, diseased old people, and the violence of poverty and profit. We have asked, petitioned, gone to courts, demonstrated peacefully, and voted for politicians full of empty promises. But we still ain't free. The time has come to defend the lives of our people against repression and for revolutionary war against the businessmen, politicians, and police. When a government

oppresses the people, we have the right to abolish it and create a new one. *Arm ourselves to defend ourselves!*[8]

The Young Lords follow in a tradition of radical action that has surfaced repeatedly in this century. It has its roots in the Nationalist Party in Puerto Rico headed by Pedro Albizú Campos in the thirties. In the wake of uprisings in several towns on the island in 1950, two New York–based Puerto Ricans allegedly tried to kill President Harry S Truman. One was shot dead and the other, Oscar Collazo, was imprisoned until his sentence was commuted in 1980. Set free at the same time were three Puerto Rican Nationalists who had sprayed bullets on the floor of the United States House of Representatives in 1954, wounding five congressmen. All vowed to continue working for independence for Puerto Rico. Acts of violence, including bombings, continue to occur on the mainland and the island.

Puerto Ricans aren't alone in wishing a change in their relationship with the United States. A Gallup poll taken in October 1979 revealed that 59 percent of United States citizens would back Puerto Rican statehood if Puerto Rico voted for it in a plebescite. On the other hand, 69 percent of United States citizens would support independence if the Puerto Ricans voted for it.

In the meantime less radical groups have also been actively working to improve the living conditions of Puerto Ricans in the United States. In

Boston, for instance, an Emergency Tenants Council composed of Puerto Ricans succeeded in getting a redevelopment plan approved by the city. The city planner said, "We've never given so much responsibility to a neighborhood group."[9]

Altogether there are more than two million Puerto Ricans living in the United States. Some have found the better life that they came for. Others are still struggling against poverty and oppression. And every year some give up that struggle and decide to return home. The trend toward reverse migration started as early as the 1960s. In 1978 twenty-seven thousand more people returned to Puerto Rico than came to the United States. For the most part they returned because they felt like strangers in their new home—outsiders for whom the American dream did not come true.

A visitor to Puerto Rico explained why Neoricans (Puerto Ricans who return from the mainland) go back home:

> . . . the desire to own a plot of land, build a house and have a collection of animals in the back is the single most compelling force in the Neoricans' lives. It is the common thread that binds them all together whenever they articulate their reasons for returning.[10]

But they also went home because they were learning to have a new sense of pride in their native island. As new economic opportunities were discovered on the island, many Puerto Ricans thought about developing their island for the first time.

But for the hundreds of thousands of Puerto Ricans who decided to stay in the United States, the struggle continues. Many still live in poverty; drug addiction and crime are common. But during the 1970s advances were made in bringing about improvements. And in New York, especially, a rich cultural life is in swing as Puerto Rican musicians, dancers, painters, and actors bring their talents to the public. Said one Puerto Rican migrant:

> Things are very, very bad for thousands of our people right now, but I am very optimistic about the future. Give us 20 years, and you'll say: "They made it—just like the Jews and Italians and everybody else who came here, struggled and won."[11]

Notes

FROM MEXICO

Chapter 1.   The Mexicans: A Conquered People

1. Rodolfo "Corky" Gonzales, *I Am Joaquín* (New York: Bantam Books, 1972).
2. Patricia De Fuentes, ed., and trans., *The Conquistadors: First-Person Accounts of the Conquest of Mexico* (New York: Orion Press, 1963), p. 181.
3. Ibid., pp. 178–180.
4. Ibid., pp. 111–112.
5. Guadalupe Vallejo, "Ranch and Mission Days in Alta California," *The Century Magazine* (December 1890), p. 183.
6. John O. Sullivan, [New York] *Morning News* (December 1845).
7. José María Sánchez, "A Trip to Texas in 1828," *Southwestern Historical Quarterly* 29 (April 1926), p. 260.
8. Miguel A. Sanchez Lamego, "To the Texas Colonists 'Mexican' Is an Execrable Word," in *Aztlan: An Anthology of Mexican American*

Literature, ed. Luis Valdez and Stan Steiner (New York: Random House, 1972), p. 92.

9. Hunter Miller, ed., *Treaties and Other International Acts of the United States of America* 5 (Washington, D.C.: Government Printing Office, 1937), p. 218.

Chapter 2. Broken Promises

1. *New York Evening Post* (December 24, 1847).
2. Josiah Royce, *California: A Study of American Character* (Boston: Houghton Mifflin, 1886), p. 363.
3. Ibid., p. 364.
4. Ibid., pp. 362–363.
5. William V. Wells, "The Quicksilver Mines of New Almaden," *Harper's New Monthly Magazine* (June 1863), p. 30.
6. John S. Hittell, "Mexican Land Claims in California," *Hutchings California Magazine* (July 1857), in *A Documentary History of the Mexican Americans,* ed. Wayne Moquin (New York: Praeger Publishers, 1971), pp. 203–204.
7. Valeska Bari, *The Cause of Empire: First Hand Accounts of California in the Days of the Gold Rush of '49* (New York: Coward-McCann, 1931), p. 54.
8. Ibid., p. 56.
9. Juan Nepomuceno Cortina, "The 'Robin Hood' of South Texas," from 36 Congress, 1 Session, House Executive Document No. 52: "Difficulties on Southwestern Frontier," in Moquin, ed., *A Documentary History,* pp. 206–209.
10. Ernesto Galarza, *Barrio Boy* (Notre Dame, Ind.: University of Notre Dame Press, 1971), p. 33.

Chapter 3.   Dreams of Freedom and Prosperity

1. Oscar Lewis, *Pedro Martínez: A Mexican Peasant and His Family* (New York: Random House, 1964), pp. 84–86.
2. Manuel Gamio, *The Mexican Immigrant: His Life Story* (Chicago: University of Chicago Press, 1931), p. 32.
3. Ibid., p. 4.
4. Ibid., p. 60.
5. Ibid., p. 7.
6. Ibid.
7. Interview with Martha Morales in *They Chose America,* An Audio Cassette Program, Vol. 1 (Princeton, N.J.: Visual Education Corp., 1975).
8. Gamio, *The Mexican Immigrant,* p. 20.
9. Interview with Martha Morales, *They Chose America.*

Chapter 4.   A Dream Turns Sour

1. Galarza, *Barrio Boy,* p. 203.
2. Ibid., p. 204.
3. Walter Woehlke, "Don't Drive Out the Mexicans," *Review of Reviews* 81 (May 1930), p. 68.
4. Paul S. Taylor, *An American-Mexican Frontier* (New York: Russell & Russell, 1934), p. 126.
5. Ibid., p. 128.
6. Galarza, *Barrio Boy,* pp. 262–263.
7. Ibid., p. 263.
8. *The Nation* 137 (September 6, 1933), p. 272.
9. Carey McWilliams, *Ill Fares the Land* (Boston: Little, Brown and Company, 1942), p. 267.
10. Ibid., pp. 267–268.
11. Ibid., p. 269.
12. Ibid., p. 273.

13. Ibid., pp. 276–277.
14. Ruth S. Camblon, "Mexicans in Chicago," *The Family* (November 1926), pp. 208–209.
15. Emory S. Bogardus, *The Mexican in the United States* (Los Angeles: University of Southern California Press, 1934), pp. 21–22.

Chapter 5. "America for the Americans"
 1. Samuel Bryan, "Mexican Immigrants in the United States," *The Survey* 28 (September 7, 1912), p. 729.
 2. Bogardus, *The Mexican in the United States,* p. 28.
 3. Charles J. and Patricia L. Bustamante, *The Mexican-American and the United States* (Mountain View, Cal.: Patty-Lar Publications, 1969), p. 34.
 4. Ibid.
 5. Robert McLean, "Goodbye, Vicente," *The Survey* 66 (May 1931), p. 182.
 6. Ruth L. Martinez, *The Unusual Mexican: A Study in Acculturation* (San Francisco: R and E Research Associates, 1973).
 7. May Lanagan, *Second Generation Mexicans in Belvedere* (master's thesis, University of Southern California, 1932), p. 17.
 8. Jacques E. Levy, *Cesar Chavez: Autobiography of La Causa* (New York: W. W. Norton, 1975), p. 24.
 9. Ibid.
10. Philip Stevenson, "Deporting Jesus," *The Nation* (July 18, 1936), p. 69.
11. Quoted in Frank Stokes, "Let the Mexicans Organize," *The Nation* (December 19, 1936), p. 731.

Chapter 6. The War Years

1. Raul Morin, *Among the Valiant* (Alhambra, Cal.: Borden Publishing Co., 1963), pp. 87–88.
2. Levy, *Cesar Chavez,* p. 84.
3. Morin, *Among the Valiant,* p. 83.
4. Ibid., pp. 61, 63.
5. Ibid., p. 60.
6. Ibid., p. 278.
7. Octavio Paz, *The Labyrinth of Solitude* (New York: Grove Press, 1961), pp. 13–14.
8. Gene L. Coon, "Pachuco," *Common Ground* 8 (Spring 1948), p. 50.
9. "In the Flow of Time," in *American Me,* ed. Beatrice Griffith (Boston: Houghton Mifflin, 1948), pp. 10–12.

Chapter 7. They Came to Work

1. Henry P. Anderson, *The Bracero Program in California* (Berkeley: University of California Press, 1961), p. 7.
2. Ibid., p. 8.
3. Ibid., p. 82.
4. *The Reporter* (February 2, 1961), p. 35.
5. Julian Samora, *Los Mojados: The Wetback Story* (Notre Dame, Ind.: University of Notre Dame Press, 1971), pp. 1–2.
6. Ibid.
7. Ibid.
8. Rinker Buck, "The New Sweatshops: A Penny for Your Collar," *New York* (January 29, 1979), p. 40.
9. Eleanor Hadley, "The Wetback Problem," *Law and Contemporary Problems* (Spring 1956), p. 345.

10. Stewart Powell, Sarah Peterson, and Juanita Hogue, "Illegal Aliens: Invasion Out of Control?" *U.S. News & World Report* (January 29, 1979), p. 41.

Chapter 8. Mexican Heritage: A New Awareness

1. Peter Matthiessen, *Sal Si Puedes* (New York: Random House, 1969), p. 126.
2. Interview with Maria Amador, *They Chose America.*
3. Cesar Chavez, Sister Mary Prudence, and Luis Valdez, "Huelga! Tales of the Delano Revolution," *Ramparts* 5 (July 1966), p. 42.
4. Reies López Tijerina, "El Grito Del Norte," in Moquin, ed., *A Documentary History,* p. 375.
5. Carlos Larralde, *Mexican American Movements and Leaders* (Los Alamitos, Cal.: Hwong Publishers, 1976).
6. David F. Gomez, *Somos Chicanos* (Boston: Beacon Press, 1973), pp. 101–102.
7. Larralde, *Mexican American Movements.*
8. Interview with Maria Amador, *They Chose America.*
9. Gomez, *Somos Chicanos.*
10. "Chicanos on the Move," *Newsweek* (January 1, 1979), p. 23.

FROM CUBA

Chapter 9. Castro Takes Over Cuba

1. Unpublished interview with Iraida Itturalde, Visual Education Corp. Archives.
2. Interview with David Sagarra, *They Chose America,* Vol. 2.

3. Interview with Lourdes Garcia, *They Chose America,* Vol. 2.
4. Ibid.
5. Ibid.

Chapter 10.   Escape to the United States

1. Richard Fagen, Richard Brody, and Thomas O'Leary, *Cubans in Exile* (Stanford, Cal.: Stanford University Press, 1968), p. 83.
2. Interview with Iraida Gil, *They Chose America,* Vol. 2.
3. Joseph P. Blank, "The Incredible Escape," *The Reader's Digest* 84 (May 1964), p. 160.
4. Interview with David Sagarra, *They Chose America,* Vol. 2.
5. Interview with Iraida Gil, *They Chose America,* Vol. 2.
6. Fagen, *et al., Cubans in Exile,* p. 79.
7. Interview with Jorge Angula, *They Chose America,* Vol. 2.
8. Blank, "The Incredible Escape," p. 160.
9. Joan Colebrook, "Key West, with Cubans," *Commentary* 56 (July 1973), p. 52.
10. Fagen, *et al., Cubans in Exile,* p. 119.
11. *Time* 93 (January 17, 1969), p. 31.
12. Frank Emmick, "An American's 14 Years in Cuban Prisons," *The New York Times* (April 12, 1978), p. A25.
13. Ibid.

Chapter 11.   Miami: A Home Away from Home

1. Quoted in John Thomas, "U.S.A. as Country of First Asylum," *International Migration,* Vol. 3, No. 1/2 (1965), p. 7.

2. Arnulfo D. Trejo, "Bicultural Americans with a Hispanic Tradition," *Wilson Library Bulletin* 44 (March 1970), p. 723.
3. Edward J. Linehan, "Cuba's Exiles Bring New Life to Miami," *National Geographic* 144 (July 1973), p. 87.
4. *American Education* (March 1965), p. 32.
5. Susan Jacoby, "Miami Si, Cuba No," *The New York Times Magazine* (September 29, 1974), p. 123.
6. Unpublished interview with Iraida Itturalde. Visual Education Corp. Archives.
7. *The New York Times* (June 9, 1980), p. B14.
8. Kathryn Johnson, "Miami: New Hispanic Power Base in U.S.," *U.S. News & World Report* (February 19, 1979), p. 69.
9. George Volsky, "Cuban Exiles Now Seek U.S. Citizenship," *The New York Times* (July 4, 1976), p. 19.
10. Jacoby, "Miami Si, Cuba No," p. 103.
11. Interview with David Sagarra, *They Chose America,* Vol. 2.
12. Interview with Iraida Gil, *They Chose America,* Vol. 2.

FROM PUERTO RICO

Chapter 12.   Puerto Ricans: Citizen Migrants

1. Jesus Colon, *A Puerto Rican in New York and Other Sketches* (New York: Mainstream Publishers, 1961), pp. 25–28.
2. Ibid.
3. Edward Mapp, *Puerto Rican Perspectives* (Metuchen, N.J.: The Scarecrow Press, 1974), p. 132.

4. Pete Hamill, "Coming of Age in Nueva York," *New York* Vol. II (November 24, 1969), in *The Puerto Rican Experience: A Sociological Sourcebook,* ed. Francesco Cordasco and Eugene Bucchioni (Totowa, N.J.: Rowman and Littlefield, 1973), p. 199.
5. Mapp, *Puerto Rican Perspectives,* p. 83.
6. Ibid.
7. Hamill, "Coming of Age . . . ," p. 201.
8. Cecyle S. Neidle, *Great Immigrants* (New York: Twayne Publishers, 1973), p. 263.
9. *The Puerto Rican Community Development Project* (New York: Puerto Rican Forum, 1964), p. 10.
10. Quoted in Francesco Cordasco, *The Puerto Ricans 1493–1973* (Dobbs Ferry, N.Y.: Oceana Publications, 1973), p. 67.

Chapter 13.   From Tarpaper Shacks to Rat-Infested Tenements
1. Piri Thomas, *Down These Mean Streets* (New York: Alfred A. Knopf, 1967), p. 24.
2. Dan Wakefield, *Island in the City: The World of Spanish Harlem* (Boston: Houghton Mifflin, 1959), p. 199.
3. Elena Padilla, *Up from Puerto Rico* (New York: Columbia University Press, 1958), p. 7.
4. Paulette Cooper, ed., *Growing up Puerto Rican* (New York: Arbor House, 1972), p. 163.
5. Patricia Cayo Sexton, *Spanish Harlem: Anatomy of Poverty* (New York: Harper & Row, 1965), p. 35.
6. Wakefield, *Island in the City,* p. 153.
7. Francesco   Cordasco   and   Diego   Castellanos,

"Teaching the Puerto Rican Experience," in *Teaching Ethnic Studies: Concepts and Strategies,* ed. James A. Banks (Washington, D.C.: National Council for the Social Studies, 1973).

8. *El Boricua: The Puerto Rican Community in Bridgeport and New Haven,* U.S. Commission on Civil Rights, Connecticut Advisory Commission, January 1973, p. 20.

9. Cooper, *Growing up Puerto Rican,* p. 156.

10. Eugene Bucchioni, "A Sociological Analysis of the Functioning of Elementary Education for Puerto Rican Children in the New York City Public Schools," unpublished doctoral dissertation in Cordasco and Bucchioni, eds., *The Puerto Rican Experience,* pp. 293–294.

Chapter 14. The Struggle Continues

1. "It's Your Turn in the Sun," *Time* (October 16, 1978), p. 58.

2. Ibid.

3. Gertrude Samuels, "A Walk Along 'the Worst Block,'" *The New York Times Magazine* (September 30, 1962), pp. 18–19.

4. Oscar Lewis, *La Vida* (New York: Random House, 1966), p. 130.

5. Gertrude Samuels, "Two Case Histories Out of Puerto Rico," *The New York Times Magazine* (January 22, 1956), p. 58.

6. Oscar Lewis, *A Study of Slum Culture: Backgrounds for La Vida* (New York: Random House, 1968), p. 183.

7. "The Puerto Ricans," *Newsweek* (June 15, 1970), p. 95.

8. "Young Lords 13-Point Program and Platform,"

in *Cracks in the Melting Pot,* ed. Melvin Steinfield (Beverly Hills, Cal.: Glencoe Press, 1973), p. 322.

9. "The Puerto Ricans," *Newsweek,* p. 96.

10. William Stockton, "Going Home: The Puerto Ricans' New Migration," *The New York Times Magazine* (November 12, 1978), p. 23.

11. "A Silent Majority Starts to Speak Out," *U.S. News & World Report* (July 13, 1970), p. 69.

Bibliography

MEXICANS

Anderson, Henry P. *The Bracero Program in California.* Berkeley: University of California Press, 1961.

Bari, Valeska. *The Cause of Empire: First Hand Accounts of California in the Days of the Gold Rush of '49.* New York: Coward-McCann, 1931.

Bogardus, Emory S. *The Mexican in the United States.* Los Angeles: University of Southern California Press, 1934.

Bryan, Samuel. "Mexican Immigrants in the United States," *The Survey* 28 (September 7, 1912).

Buck, Rinker. "The New Sweatshops: A Penny for Your Collar," *New York,* January 29, 1979.

Bustamante, Charles J., and Patricia L. Bustamante. *The Mexican-American and the United States.* Mountain View, Calif.: Patty-Lar Publications, 1969.

Camblon, Ruth S. "Mexicans in Chicago," *The Family,* November 1926.

146 Bibliography

Chavez, Cesar, Sister Mary Prudence, and Luis Valdez. "Huelga! Tales of the Delano Revolution," *Ramparts* 5 (July 1966).

"Chicanos on the Move," *Newsweek,* January 1, 1979.

Coon, Gene L. "Pachuco," *Common Ground* 8 (Spring 1948).

Cortina, Juan Nepomuceno. "The 'Robin Hood' of South Texas," from 36 Congress, 1 Session, House Executive Document No. 52: "Difficulties on Southwestern Frontier," in Moquin, ed., *A Documentary History. Which see.*

De Fuentes, Patricia, ed., and trans. *The Conquistadors: First-Person Accounts of the Conquest of Mexico.* New York: Orion Press, 1963.

Galarza, Ernesto. *Barrio Boy.* Notre Dame, Ind.: University of Notre Dame Press, 1971.

Gamio, Manuel. *The Mexican Immigrant: His Life Story.* Chicago: University of Chicago Press, 1931.

Gomez, David F., *Somos Chicanos.* Boston: Beacon Press, 1973.

Gonzales, Rodolfo "Corky." *I Am Joaquín.* New York: Bantam Books, 1972.

Griffith, Beatrice, ed. "In the Flow of Time," in *American Me.* Boston: Houghton Mifflin, 1948.

Hadley, Eleanor. "The Wetback Problem," *Law and Contemporary Problems,* (Spring 1956).

Hittell, John S. "Mexican Land Claims in California," *Hutchings California Magazine,* July 1857, in Moquin, ed., *A Documentary History. Which see.*

Jones, Solomon. *The Government Riots of Los Angeles, June 1943.* San Francisco, Calif.: R and E Research Associates, 1973.

Lamego, Miguel A. Sanchez. "To the Texas Colonists 'Mexican' Is an Execrable Word," in Valdez and Steiner, eds., *Aztlan: An Anthology. Which see.*

Lanagan, May. *Second Generation Mexicans in Belvedere.* Master's thesis, University of Southern California, 1932.

Levy, Jacques E. *Cesar Chavez: Autobiography of La Causa.* New York: W. W. Norton, 1975.

Lewis, Oscar. *Pedro Martínez: A Mexican Peasant and His Family.* New York: Random House, 1964.

Martinez, Ruth L. *The Unusual Mexican: A Study in Acculturation.* San Francisco, Calif.: R and E Research Associates, 1973.

Matthiessen, Peter. *Sal Si Puedes.* New York: Random House, 1969.

McLean, Robert. "Goodbye, Vicente," *The Survey* 66 (May 1931).

McWilliams, Carey. *Ill Fares the Land.* Boston: Little, Brown and Company, 1942.

Miller, Hunter, ed. *Treaties and Other International Acts of the United States of America* 5. Washington, D.C.: Government Printing Office, 1937.

Moquin, Wayne, ed. *A Documentary History of the Mexican Americans.* New York: Praeger Publishers, 1971.

Morin, Raul. *Among the Valiant.* Alhambra, Calif.: Borden Publishing Co., 1963.

The Nation 137 (September 6, 1933).

New York Evening Post, December 24, 1847.

Paz, Octavio. *The Labyrinth of Solitude.* New York: Grove Press, 1961.

Powell, Stewart, Sarah Peterson, and Juanita Hogue. "Illegal Aliens: Invasion Out of Control?" *U.S. News & World Report,* January 29, 1979.

The Reporter, February 2, 1961.

Royce, Josiah. *California: A Study of American Character.* Boston: Houghton Mifflin, 1886.

Samora, Julian. *Los Mojados: The Wetback Story.* Notre Dame, Ind.: University of Notre Dame Press, 1971.

Sánchez, José María. "A Trip to Texas in 1828," *Southwestern Historical Quarterly* 29 (April 1926).

Stevenson, Philip. "Deporting Jesus," *The Nation,* July 18, 1936.

Stokes, Frank. "Let the Mexicans Organize!" *The Nation,* December 19, 1936.

Sullivan, John O. [New York] *Morning News,* December 1845.

Taylor, Paul S. *An American-Mexican Frontier.* New York: Russell & Russell, 1934.

Tijerina, Reies López. *El Grito Del Norte,* in Moquin, ed., *A Documentary History. Which see.*

Valdez, Luis and Stan Steiner, eds. *Aztlan: An Anthology of Mexican American Literature.* New York: Random House, 1972.

Vallejo, Guadalupe. "Ranch and Mission Days in Alta California," *The Century Magazine,* December 1890.

Wells, William V. "The Quicksilver Mines of New Almaden," *Harper's New Monthly Magazine,* June 1863.

Woehlke, Walter. "Don't Drive Out the Mexicans," *Review of Reviews* 81 (May 1930).

Audio Program

They Chose America, Vol. 1. An Audio Cassette Program. Princeton, N.J.: Visual Education Corp., 1975.

CUBANS

American Education, March 1965.

Blank, Joseph P. "The Incredible Escape," *The Reader's Digest* 84 (May 1964).

Colebrook, Joan. "Key West, with Cubans," *Commentary* 56 (July 1973).

Emmick, Frank. "An American's 14 Years in Cuban Prisons," *The New York Times,* April 12, 1978.

Fagen, Richard, Richard Brody, and Thomas O'Leary. *Cubans in Exile.* Stanford, Calif.: Stanford University Press, 1968.

Jacoby, Susan. "Miami Si, Cuba No," *The New York Times Magazine,* September 29, 1974.

Johnson, Kathryn. "Miami: New Hispanic Power Base in U.S.," *U.S. News & World Report,* February 19, 1979.

Linehan, Edward J. "Cuba's Exiles Bring New Life to Miami," *National Geographic* 144 (July 1973).

The New York Times, June 9, 1980.

Ramírez, Armando Socarras, as told to Denis Fodor and John Reddy. "Stowaway," *The Reader's Digest,* January 1970.

Thomas, John. "U.S.A. as Country of First Asylum," *International Migration,* Vol. 3 No. 1/2 (1965).

Time 93 (January 17, 1969).

Trejo, Arnulfo D. "Bicultural Americans with a Hispanic Tradition," *Wilson Library Bulletin* 44 (March 1970).

Van Gelder, Lawrence. "Exile's Road to Past Is a Cuban Revelation," *The New York Times,* April 16, 1978.

Volsky, George. "Cuban Exiles Now Seek U.S. Citizenship," *The New York Times,* July 4, 1976.

Additional Readings

Nicholson, Joe Jr. *Inside Cuba.* New York: Sheed and Ward, Inc., 1974.

Plank, John, ed. *Cuba and the United States: Long Range Perspectives.* Washington, D.C.: The Brookings Institution, 1967.

Radosh, Ronald, ed. *The New Cuba: Paradoxes and Potentials.* New York: William Morrow & Co., Inc., 1976.

Smith, Robert F. *The United States and Cuba: Business and Diplomacy, 1917–1960.* New York: Bookman Assoc., 1960.

Williams, William Appleman. *The United States, Cuba and Castro.* New York: Monthly Review Press, 1962.

Yglesias, José. *In the Fist of the Revolution: Life in a Cuban Country Town.* New York: Pantheon Books, 1968.

Audio Program

They Chose America, Vol. 2. An Audio Cassette Program. Princeton, N.J.: Visual Education Corp., 1975.

PUERTO RICANS

"A Silent Minority Starts to Speak Out," *U.S. News & World Report,* July 13, 1970.

Banks, James A., ed. *Teaching Ethnic Studies: Concepts and Strategies.* Washington, D.C.: National Council for the Social Studies, 1973.

Bucchioni, Eugene. "A Sociological Analysis of the Functioning of Elementary Education for Puerto Rican Children in the New York City Public Schools." Unpublished doctoral dissertation in

Cordasco and Bucchioni, eds., *The Puerto Rican Experience. Which see.*

Colon, Jesus. *A Puerto Rican in New York and Other Sketches.* New York: Mainstream Publishers, 1961.

Cooper, Paulette, ed. *Growing up Puerto Rican.* New York: Arbor House, 1972.

Cordasco, Francesco. *The Puerto Ricans 1493–1973.* Dobbs Ferry, N.Y.: Oceana Publications, 1973.

Cordasco, Francesco, and Eugene Bucchioni, eds. *The Puerto Rican Experience: A Sociological Sourcebook.* Totowa, N.J.: Rowman and Littlefield, 1973.

Cordasco, Francesco, and Diego Castellanos. "Teaching the Puerto Rican Experience," in Banks, ed., *Teaching Ethnic Studies. Which see.*

El Boricua: The Puerto Rican Community in Bridgeport and New Haven. U.S. Commission on Civil Rights, Connecticut Advisory Commission, January, 1973.

Hamill, Pete. "Coming of Age in Nueva York," in Cordasco and Bucchioni, eds., *The Puerto Rican Experience. Which see.*

"It's Your Turn in the Sun," *Time,* October 16, 1978.

Lewis, Oscar. *La Vida.* New York: Random House, 1966.

———. *A Study of Slum Clearance Backgrounds for La Vida.* New York: Random House, 1968.

Mapp, Edward. *Puerto Rican Perspectives.* Metuchen, N.J.: The Scarecrow Press, 1974.

Moreau, John Adams. "The Puerto Ricans: Who Are They?", in Wagenheim, ed., *The Puerto Ricans. Which see.*

Neidle, Cecyle S. *Great Immigrants.* New York: Twayne Publishers, 1973.

New York Post, October 7, 1972.

Padilla, Elena. *Up from Puerto Rico.* New York: Columbia University Press, 1958.

"The Puerto Ricans," *Newsweek,* June 15, 1970.

The Puerto Rican Community Development Project. New York: Puerto Rican Forum, 1964.

Samuels, Gertrude. "Two Case Histories Out of Puerto Rico," *The New York Times Magazine,* January 22, 1956.

————. "A Walk Along 'the Worst Block,' " *The New York Times Magazine,* September 30, 1962.

Sexton, Patricia Cayo. *Spanish Harlem: Anatomy of Poverty.* New York: Harper & Row, 1965.

Sheehan, Susan. "A Welfare Mother," *The New Yorker,* September 29, 1975.

Shorris, Earl. "Spanish Harlem," *Harper's,* June 1978.

Steinfield, Melvin, ed. *Cracks in the Melting Pot.* Beverly Hills, Calif.: Glencoe Press, 1973.

Stockton, William. "Going Home: The Puerto Ricans' New Migration," *The New York Times Magazine,* November 12, 1978.

Thomas, Piri. *Down These Mean Streets.* New York: Alfred A. Knopf, 1967.

Wagenheim, Kal, ed. *The Puerto Ricans: A Documentary History.* New York: Praeger Publishers, 1973.

Wakefield, Dan. *Island in the City: The World of Spanish Harlem.* Boston: Houghton Mifflin, 1959.

————. "The Other Puerto Ricans," *The New York Times Magazine,* October 11, 1959.

"Young Lords 13-Point Program and Platform," in Steinfield, ed., *Cracks in the Melting Pot. Which see.*

A Brief History of U.S. Immigration Laws

The authority to formulate immigration policy rests with Congress and is contained in Article 1, Section 8, Clause 3 of the Constitution, which provides that Congress shall have the power to "regulate commerce with foreign nations, and among the several States, and with the Indian tribes."

Alien Act of 1798: authorized the deportation of aliens by the President. Expired after two years.

For the next seventy-five years there was no federal legislation restricting admission to, or allowing deportation from, the United States.

Act of 1875: excluded criminals and prostitutes and entrusted inspection of immigrants to collectors of the ports.

Act of 1882: excluded lunatics and idiots and persons liable to becoming a public charge.

First Chinese Exclusion Act.

Acts of 1885 and 1887: contract labor laws, which made it unlawful to import aliens under contract for labor or services of any kind. (Exceptions: artists, lecturers, servants, skilled aliens in an industry not yet established in the United States, etc.)

Act of 1888: amended previous acts to provide for expulsion of aliens landing in violation of contract laws.

153

Act of 1891: first exclusion of persons with certain diseases; felons, also persons having committed crimes involving moral turpitude; polygamists, etc.

Act of 1903: further exclusion of persons with certain mental diseases, epilepsy, etc.; beggars; also "anarchists or persons who believe in, or advocate the overthrow by force or violence of the Government of the United States or of all government or of all forms of law or the assassination of public officials." Further refined deportation laws.

Acts of 1907, 1908: further exclusions for health reasons, such as TB.

Exclusion of persons detrimental to labor conditions in the United States, specifically Japanese and Korean skilled or unskilled laborers.

Gentlemen's Agreement with Japan: in which Japan agreed to restrictions imposed by the United States.

Act of 1917: codified previous exclusion provisions, and added literacy test. Further restricted entry of other Asians.

Act of 1921: First Quota Law, in which approximately 350,000 immigrants were permitted entry, mostly from northern or western Europe.

Act of 1924: National Origins Quota System set annual limitations on the number of aliens of any nationality immigrating to the U.S. The act also decreed, in a provision aimed primarily at the Japanese, that no alien ineligible for citizenship could be admitted to the U.S.

"Gigolo Act" of 1937: allowing deportation of aliens fraudulently marrying in order to enter the United States either by having marriage annulled or by refusing to marry once having entered the country.

Act of 1940: Alien Registration Act provided for registration and fingerprinting of all aliens.

Act of 1943: Chinese Exclusion Acts repealed.

Act of 1945: War Brides Act admitted during the three years of act's existence approximately 118,000 brides, grooms, and children of servicemen who had married foreign nationals during World War II.

Act of 1949: Displaced Persons Act admitted more than four hundred thousand people displaced as a result of World War II (to 1952).

Act of 1950: Internal Security Act excluded from immigrating any present or foreign member of the Communist party, and made more easily deportable people of this class already in the U.S. Also provided for alien registration by January 10 of each year.

Act of 1952: Immigration and Nationality Act codified all existing legislation; also eliminated race as a bar to immigration.

Acts of 1953–1956: Refugee Relief acts admitted orphans, Hungarians after 1956 uprising, skilled sheepherders.

1957: special legislation to admit Hungarian refugees.

1960: special legislation paroled Cuban refugees into the U.S.

Act of 1965: legislation amending act of 1952 phased out national origins quotas by 1968, with new numerical ceilings on a first come, first served basis. Numerical ceilings (per annum): 120,000 for natives of the Western Hemisphere; 170,000 for natives of the Eastern Hemisphere. New preference categories: relatives (74 percent), scientists, artists (10 percent), skilled and unskilled labor (10 percent), refugees (6 percent).

Act of 1977: allowed Indo-Chinese who had been paroled into the U.S. to adjust their status to permanent resident.

1979: Presidential directive allowed thousands of Vietnamese "boat people" to enter the U.S.

1980: Presidential directive allowed some 125,000 Cubans to enter the U.S. as political refugees.

Index